P. M. C. S.

PREVENTIVE MAINTENANCE FOR COUPLES'
SUCCESS

AIGBEFO D DOMINION

Paperback ISBN: 978-1-968464-00-4

eBook ISBN: 979-8-9860017-9-1

Library of Congress Control Number: 2025911547

Published by Aishific Press.

Aishific Press

Visit www.aisificpress.com.

books@aishific.com; 1 (352) 300 6373

Printed and bound in the United States of America.

First Printing, 2025

To my wife and life partner,
whose unwavering love, prayers, and companionship reflect the
very essence of this book, thank you for walking this journey
with me.
To couples everywhere who choose commitment over convenience,
this work is for you.

And ultimately,
To God, our covenant-keeping Father,
The source of every insight, restoration, and enduring love.

ACKNOWLEDGMENTS

I am deeply grateful to God for the vision, grace, and strength that enabled me to complete this book. His wisdom has been my anchor throughout this journey.

To my family, thank you for your patience, encouragement, and belief in the message of marriage as a sacred covenant.

To the countless couples, soldiers, counselors, and chaplains who have shared their stories, struggles, and victories with me, you have inspired much of what is written on these pages.

To my editors, design team, and support network—thank you for your excellence, creativity, and attention to detail.

To every reader, may this book serve as a tool of hope, guidance, and transformation in your marriage journey.

Prevention is better than a cure; let this be your story.

CONTENTS

Introduction   ix

1. What is a Good Marriage?   1
2. Building a Strong Foundation   13
3. Relationship Maintenance   25
4. Regular Relationship Check-ups   45
5. Communication: A Preventive Tool   61
6. Marital Conflict Resolution   75
7. Relational Gratitude   97
8. Love Beyond Transactions   113
9. Intimacy: A Sacred Aspect of Marriage   133
10. Financial Intimacy in Marriage   149
11. Restoring Intimacy After Hurt 1   173
12. Restoring Intimacy After Hurt 2   193
13. Maintaining Intimacy and Protecting Your Union   209
14. Forgiveness and Rebuilding Trust in Marriage   223
15. Serving One Another   241
16. Faith Strengthens Marriage   253
17. Leaving a Lasting Legacy   265
    Final Words & Encouragement   275

COUPLES RECONNECTION PLAN   279
30-Day Marriage Reconnection Challenge   287
Appendices & Bonus Content   293
Reference List   301
About the Author   307
More from the Author   309

INTRODUCTION

Marriage, one of life's most profound and meaningful relationships, is a sacred union that beautifully reflects God's unconditional love for His people. It symbolizes the covenant between Christ and the Church. Maintaining a healthy and lasting marriage, similar to caring for a well-maintained vehicle or military gear, demands consistent and deliberate effort. However, the happiness and fulfillment derived from a successful marriage are truly unmatched. This is the heart of Preventive Maintenance for Couples' Success (PMCS). Embracing this proactive approach fosters deeper connection, resilience, and joy in the marital journey, reminding us that caring for love daily is the key to building a lasting and fulfilling marriage.

WHY P.M.C.S.?

In military operations, Preventive Maintenance Checks and Services (PMCS) serve as the vital backbone for keeping vehicles and equipment in optimal working condition. Soldiers are rigorously trained to inspect, identify, and address potential issues proactively, preventing problems from escalating into significant failures. This proactive approach empowers them, giving them control over the situation. Similarly, marriage benefits immensely from preventative care, giving couples the confidence that they can handle any challenge that comes their way.

Waiting until issues become evident often results in unnecessary pain, resentment, and brokenness. Through regular check-ins, such as weekly or monthly discussions about the state of the relationship, open communication, and proactive attention, like planning regular date nights or surprise gestures of love, couples can navigate common pitfalls that threaten satisfaction and stability, ultimately fostering a resilient and thriving relationship. This book is crafted as a practical guide designed to help you apply these essential principles to your relationship. Whether you are newly married, a seasoned couple, or facing the unique challenges of military life, PMCS provides powerful strategies to nurture and sustain a strong, enduring marriage.

MARRIAGE AS A COVENANT, NOT A CONTRACT

Within the PMCS framework, one of the most vital distinctions is viewing marriage as a sacred covenant rather than a contractual agreement. Unlike a contract, which is based on specific terms and conditions that each party is obligated to fulfill, a covenant embodies an unwavering commitment that endures regardless of circumstances. The Bible vividly depicts marriage as a sacred covenant (Malachi 2:14), emphasizing that it surpasses mere convenience or personal happiness. Instead, marriage is a divine union that reflects God's glory and sanctifies both partners. In Ephesians 5:25-28, the apostle Paul further elaborates on this, instructing husbands to love their wives as Christ loved the church, sacrificially and selflessly, and wives to respect their husbands, demonstrating trust in God's divine design.

This profound covenant calls husbands and wives to embody a deep sense of oneness, demonstrating Christlike love, respect, submission, and grace. Such a relationship cultivates a bond rooted in divine purpose and unwavering devotion, inspiring couples to pursue a marriage characterized by love that is steadfast and transcendent. This understanding elevates marriage from a mere social contract to a sacred, divine purpose, calling us to honor it as a reflection of God's eternal love.

PREVENTION IS BETTER THAN A CURE

Disagreements, unmet expectations, and emotional disconnection are natural and inevitable aspects of any marriage. However, the key to a healthy relationship lies in how couples handle these challenges. Many couples fall into the trap of waiting until problems become overwhelming before seeking help, which can lead to unnecessary pain and strain. This reactive approach often allows hurt and resentment to take root, making the issues more difficult to resolve.

Instead, preventive maintenance offers a robust, proactive strategy. By regularly assessing the health of your relationship and addressing concerns early on, you can prevent minor disagreements from spiraling into full-blown crises. This proactive care not only preserves love and understanding but also strengthens your bond. It enables your marriage to weather life's inevitable storms while emerging even stronger. Passionately investing in preventive efforts transforms a marriage from merely surviving to truly flourishing, cultivating a deep connection that stands the test of time.

A KINGDOM PERSPECTIVE ON MARRIAGE

The principles outlined in this book are deeply rooted in biblical truths and kingdom values, offering a timeless perspective on marriage. In today's society, the popular notion is to marry for love, compatibility, or friendship; however, the Bible presents a different and profound view. It teaches us that the focus should be on loving the person we marry, rather than simply marrying someone we already love. Love, according to Scripture, is more than an emotion; it's a deliberate action that involves serving, forgiving, and sacrificing for one another with a genuine heart. This is what we refer to as 'divine love', a love that mirrors the sacrificial love of Christ for the Church.

Ephesians 5:25-28 emphasizes this divine love, instructing husbands to love their wives as Christ loved the church, sacrificially and selflessly. Wives, in turn, are called to respect their husbands, demonstrating trust in God's divine design. When these roles are embraced with sincerity and passion, they cultivate a harmonious and mutually fulfilling partnership. Such unity and love not only strengthen the marriage bond but also reflect the divine love of Christ, inspiring couples to build their relationships on a foundation of grace, sacrifice, and unwavering commitment.

WHAT TO EXPECT FROM THIS BOOK

This book is thoughtfully organized into five interconnected parts, each crafted to reinforce the core principles of preventive maintenance for couples committed to nurturing a strong, loving marriage. It aims to inspire couples to actively invest in their relationship, fostering growth, resilience, and deep connection.

Part I: Foundations of a Healthy Relationship— Begin your journey by exploring the biblical roots and practical aspects of marriage. Delve into shared values, mutual respect, and the vital roles of love, submission, and leadership. These elements form the bedrock of a resilient and harmonious partnership, emphasizing that a solid foundation is essential for enduring love. This emphasis on mutual respect and understanding makes each partner feel valued and respected, strengthening the bond of the marriage.

Part II: Preventive Maintenance Strategies — Discover powerful, actionable tools to keep your relationship vibrant and fulfilling. Focus on enhancing effective communication, deepening emotional and physical intimacy, and skillfully balancing responsibilities. These strategies are designed to cultivate harmony, understanding, and proactive care within your marriage.

Part III: Navigating Challenges Together— Learn how to gracefully face life's inevitable transitions, conflicts, and unmet expectations. Embracing forgiveness and proactive planning becomes vital in strengthening your bond during difficult times, turning challenges into opportunities for growth and deeper connection.

Part IV: Sustaining a Thriving Marriage— Find inspiration in celebrating milestones, growing spiritually as a couple, and creating a meaningful legacy of love. This section encourages you to nurture your relationship in ways that ensure its vitality and relevance across generations.

Part V: Preventive Maintenance in Action— Apply what you've learned through practical, tailored check-ups—daily, weekly, monthly, and yearly. Each chapter offers practical activities, conversation starters, and biblical insights, empowering you and your spouse to deepen your connection intentionally. This guide is designed to be flexible, encouraging you to adapt and personalize your approach so your relationship can flourish and withstand life's changes. Embark on this journey with passion and purpose, confident that committed, intentional care lays the foundation for a lasting, fulfilling marriage. Every step taken in love and awareness brings you closer to a relationship built to last and flourish.

How to Use This Book

This book is designed as both a resource and a workbook. It contains reflective questions, actionable steps, and real-life applications. Whether you work through it individually or with your spouse, take your time with each chapter, allowing space for reflection and growth. The activities provided are designed to encourage open communication, intimacy, and mutual support, thereby fostering a more profound connection in your marriage.

A Call to Commitment

Marriage is not a destination but a journey filled with opportunities to grow, learn, and become more like Christ. By embracing preventive maintenance, you are committing to prioritizing your relationship, honoring your covenant, and glorifying God through your union.

 It won't always be easy, but it will be worth it. Every effort you invest in your marriage, every step you take towards a stronger foundation, a deeper connection, and a legacy of love that extends beyond your lifetime, is worth it. Your journey is valid, and your commitment is reassuring.

Let's begin this journey together. Turn the page and start building a marriage that not only survives but thrives, not by chance, but by God's design. The joy of seeing your relationship grow and flourish is a beautiful reward for your commitment and effort.

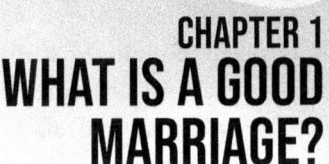

CHAPTER 1

WHAT IS A GOOD MARRIAGE?

A good marriage is fundamentally a partnership grounded in love, trust, respect, and mutual understanding. It entails open communication, effective conflict resolution, and a joint commitment to each other's happiness and personal growth. In such marriages, both partners actively support and encourage one another while preserving their identities and interests.

The essence of a fulfilling marriage lies in emotional connection, intimacy, and companionship, as well as the joy and profound satisfaction it brings. This joy and satisfaction are a continuous stream that nourishes the relationship. While every marriage is unique, the hallmark of a healthy marriage is its capacity to provide lasting happiness, emotional safety, and fulfillment for both partners, offering a beacon of hope and optimism.

A GOOD MARRIAGE IS A PRODUCT OF COMMITMENT

At the heart of every successful marriage lies an unwavering commitment, a foundational pillar that supports the entire relationship. This commitment is not merely a fleeting emotion but a deliberate and ongoing choice that requires couples to prioritize their bond above all else. It is an invitation to journey together through life's myriad challenges, celebrating the joyful moments while maneuvering through obstacles hand in hand. This commitment serves as the anchor that keeps the relationship steady, even in the stormiest of times, providing both partners with a sense of security and reassurance.

When partners dedicate themselves to this journey, they cultivate an environment where love, trust, and understanding can thrive. This steadfast dedication is a bedrock, enabling both individuals to grow and evolve while remaining intimately connected. Marriages fortified by such unwavering commitment are resilient and poised to withstand life's inevitable trials. Through continuous effort and shared resolve, couples can build a stable, lasting partnership that stands the test of time and deepens with each passing day. As they navigate life together, their bond becomes a testament to the power of commitment, illustrating how two hearts, united in purpose, can create a love that endures.

A GOOD MARRIAGE HAS NO EXIT STRATEGY OR PLAN B

In a genuinely flourishing marriage, the notion of an exit strategy or a "plan B" is entirely absent. An exit strategy in marriage refers to having a backup plan or an alternative route in case the relationship encounters difficulties. When partners approach their union with this mindset, it fundamentally undermines the profound commitment to authentic intimacy and resilience.

Instead, couples should view challenges as valuable opportunities to deepen their connection and fortify their bond. By working together to navigate difficulties, they cultivate a spirit of collaboration and perseverance, reinforcing their relationship rather than seeking convenient exits.

This unwavering mindset eradicates any thoughts of contingency plans, compelling both partners to dedicate their entire emotional, mental, and spiritual energy to nurturing and safeguarding their union. It fosters trust and assurance, inviting individuals to invest in their shared life, where each thread symbolizes love, growth, and commitment. In this sacred space, they embrace the journey of marriage, not as a destination with an alternative route but as an evolving adventure they undertake together, come what may.

A GOOD MARRIAGE IS NOT A PRODUCT OF LOVE ALONE

While love undoubtedly serves as the foundation of a romantic relationship, it alone is insufficient to sustain a thriving marriage. A healthy and enduring marital bond also hinges on a collection of vital elements: unwavering commitment, deep-seated trust, and the art of effective communication. These pillars are complemented by mutual respect, shared values, and an earnest willingness to resolve conflicts constructively.

This mutual respect is not just a courtesy but a deep acknowledgment of each other's worth. It is a commitment to treat each other with dignity and honor. Mutual respect makes both partners feel valued and respected. Love ignites the initial connection as it envelops couples in emotional warmth and passion. Mutual respect, on the other hand, is one of the additional factors that act as essential reinforcements. Over time, it diligently fortifies the relationship against the inevitable trials of life.

The daily practice of love, with the pillars and vital elements, is a shared responsibility that enhances love in the marriage. This shared responsibility matures their relationship.

It empowers their marital survival and flourishing. As a result, they built a resilient partnership that stands the test of time.

A GOOD MARRIAGE IS NOT A PRODUCT OF PRAYER ALONE

In the intricate fabric of a successful marriage, prayer undoubtedly weaves a thread of profound importance and spiritual depth. For many couples, it serves as a wellspring of comfort and divine guidance, fostering a connection that transcends the everyday hustle and bustle. When God stands at the heart of a marriage, both partners find themselves drawn closer to Him and, in turn, to each other. This sacred bond transforms into something deeply substantial and enduring.

However, it is crucial to recognize that depending solely on prayer, without any active effort, proves insufficient for nurturing a vibrant partnership. It is akin to having heartfelt conversations with God, yet neglecting to embody His teachings within the four walls of your home. Some might mistakenly believe that if they pray for their marriage, God will magically smooth over their shortcomings without any personal initiative for change.

Intentional effort becomes paramount to cultivating a thriving marriage. This entails fostering open lines of communication, demonstrating mutual respect, engaging in practical problem-solving, and collaborating as a team. While prayer is a powerful support system that can elevate these endeavors, it cannot replace the daily acts of love. It cannot replace the commitment essential for nurturing a resilient marital bond.

 A successful marriage is shaped through prayer, a balanced combination of spiritual devotion and active involvement in the relationship.

A GOOD MARRIAGE IS NOT A PRODUCT OF SEX ALONE

While physical intimacy plays a crucial role in fostering a healthy and satisfying marriage, it is far from the only element contributing to its strength and vitality. Deep emotional connection, open and effective communication, unwavering trust, companionship, and a profound mutual understanding form the foundation for successful marriages.

When partners share an emotional bond, they create a safe haven where both can express their thoughts and feelings without fear of judgment. This sense of support and connection enhances their physical intimacy and overall satisfaction within the marriage. Sexual intimacy, while significant, is merely one element in the beautifully intricate fabric of marital life.

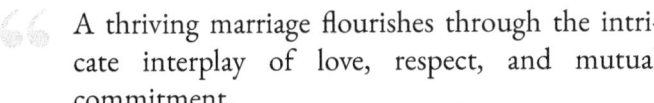 A thriving marriage flourishes through the intricate interplay of love, respect, and mutual commitment.

This evidence suggests that the true essence of partnership extends far beyond the physical dimension. This blend of emotional closeness and shared experiences truly nurtures the heart of a successful marriage.

A GOOD MARRIAGE IS NOT A PRODUCT OF A SUCCESSFUL "TEST DRIVE"

In today's fast-paced society, the notion of "test-driving" relationships has gained traction, with many advocating for couples to cohabit or engage in sexual intimacy before tying the knot. This idea, however enticing it may seem, often lacks the foundation for a genuine long-term commitment. Just as consumers might try out various products before making a purchase, this superficial evaluation can lead to a transient outlook on love and partnership, diluting the profound commitment that marriage requires.

Instead of fostering deep connections, "test-driving" relationships can create a mindset that values temporary satisfaction over enduring loyalty. The essence of a strong marriage lies not in preliminary trials but in shared values, mutual dedication, and the continuous journey of growth together. The blend of trust, open communication, and unwavering support beautifully weaves together the fabric of a strong marriage, creating a partnership that flourishes well beyond the initial excitement of compatibility checks. Genuine marital stability stems from the dedication to face life's challenges together. It is a commitment to nurturing a life filled with meaning and depth, rather than relying on surface-level evaluations of a trial run.

A GOOD MARRIAGE IS NOT ABOUT MONEY OR COMFORT ALONE

While financial stability and a comfortable lifestyle can ease many of life's burdens, they are not enough to build a fulfilling marriage. When relationships are mainly based on financial security or the appeal of a luxurious lifestyle, they risk becoming transactional. This removes the genuine emotional intimacy and the vital depth needed for lasting love. Imagine a relationship thriving on laughter, shared dreams, and mutual understanding, yet feeling empty when it relies solely on material wealth.

Financial prosperity without emotional connection, mutual respect, and aligned goals often leads to a deep sense of emptiness. It's like a beautifully decorated house that feels hollow inside because it lacks any human presence. Conversely, a truly fulfilling marriage combines wise financial decisions with strong emotional bonds, lasting trust, unwavering support, and a shared sense of spirituality. This kind of partnership thrives on shared resources and a deep bond that elevates both partners, making their journey together even more meaningful.

A SUCCESSFUL MARRIAGE IS NOT 50/50; IT IS 100/100

The widespread notion that a marriage is founded on equal contributions, often summed up as the "50/50" approach, implies that each partner only needs to meet the other halfway. However, a truly thriving and meaningful marriage calls for something far more profound. Both partners must pour their entire selves into the relationship, with 100% commitment from each side. This entails being fully present and dedicated to the relationship every single day. Active presence and dedication are seen through small acts of kindness, supportive gestures, and even significant sacrifices that openly demonstrate genuine devotion and love. This means actively seeking opportunities to outdo one another in expressions of love, without any form of competition or comparison.

In these moments of authentic commitment and presence, couples forge a resilient and enduring connection, one strengthened by a remarkable sense of unity. When each partner wholeheartedly embraces this ideal of total contribution, they create not just a marriage but an unbreakable bond. They make a union, one capable of weathering any storm life may bring and emerging stronger each time, united by their shared dedication.

A GOOD MARRIAGE IS NOT ABOUT HAVING KIDS ALONE

Children are genuinely a treasured blessing, infusing a marriage with boundless joy, deep-seated purpose, and vibrant energy. Their presence not only enriches the familial fabric but also strengthens the emotional bonds between partners, creating shared moments of happiness that serve as cornerstones for a resilient relationship. The arrival of children can invigorate a marriage, fostering a sense of collective purpose and unity as couples watch their offspring grow and thrive. These shared experiences often deepen the emotional connection, creating a cascade of memories that nourish the partnership and strengthen their bond.

However, it is vital to understand that a successful and enduring marriage does not depend exclusively on the factors of parenthood. While children can add layers of happiness and fulfillment, the foundation of a robust marriage must be built upon the pillars of mutual love, respect, understanding, and ongoing support. Couples should dedicate time and effort to cultivating a strong, loving relationship that is independent of their roles as parents, ensuring that their partnership remains resilient even without the presence of children.

Relying solely on parenthood for marital stability can be a risky approach. As children grow older, seek independence, and eventually leave the nest, the couple's relationship may face unexpected strain if it was predominantly centered on parenting roles. Without a solid personal connection, the departure of children can leave a void, making the marriage vulnerable to challenges and misunderstandings. Such marriages may become strained or fragile, especially if the emotional connection was primarily defined by parental responsibilities rather than genuine companionship.

To foster a resilient and fulfilling marriage, couples should focus on developing qualities that promote long-term stability and happiness. These include cultivating intimacy, a deep emotional closeness that allows both partners to feel seen and understood, building heartfelt connections through open communication and shared experiences, and establishing common goals and visions for the future. Pursuing shared dreams and supporting each other's personal growth not only enhances mutual satisfaction but also creates a sense of partnership that endures beyond the immediate joys of parenthood.

Furthermore, nurturing a marriage with these qualities helps couples navigate life's inevitable challenges, whether personal, professional, or familial, more effectively. When the relationship is rooted in genuine companionship and aligned in purpose, it remains vibrant and resilient, capable of withstanding the tests of time and change. Whether or not children are part of the equation, these foundational elements serve as the bedrock for a joyful, supportive, and lasting union, ensuring that both partners continue to find fulfillment and connection throughout their lives together.

A GOOD MARRIAGE IS NOT ABOUT CURING YOUR LONELINESS

Many individuals enter marriage hopeful that it will eliminate their feelings of loneliness. While marriage can indeed foster companionship and create opportunities for emotional connection, it should not be viewed as a guaranteed cure for deep-seated personal loneliness or emotional emptiness. A truly thriving marriage is built on a foundation of two emotionally mature individuals who have worked to cultivate their sense of fulfillment, self-awareness, and happiness before committing to a shared life. Relying solely on marriage to alleviate loneliness can impose unnecessary pressure on the relationship, often leading to disappointment and emotional strain that threaten the bond between partners. This mindset can also hinder both individuals from fully addressing their own emotional needs, which are crucial for genuine intimacy.

A successful marriage flourishes when both partners are emotionally whole and also when they are on the path of fulfilment or fulfilled in their individual lives. Each brings their unique joys, challenges, and aspirations into the relationship. When couples approach their relationship as a shared journey of growth, rather than as a mere refuge from loneliness, they flourish. Such partnerships foster continuous growth, deepening understanding, and resilience, emphasizing the importance of individual well-being alongside the union.

A GOOD MARRIAGE PLACES COLLECTIVE COMMITMENT OVER PERSONAL GRATIFICATION

In today's culture, marriage is often seen as a refuge for financial stability and emotional security. Many overlook the complex partnership that defines this sacred bond. In a truly fulfilling marriage, the focus shifts from individual desires to a shared commitment. Each partner prioritizes the health of their union, guided by the solemn vows they made to each other. This covenant goes beyond personal satisfaction. It reflects a deeper commitment to selflessness and spiritual growth.

The biblical model highlights that marriage is not just about companionship. It is not merely for personal satisfaction; it is a profound journey. This sacred union shapes both individuals into reflections of Christ's love and grace. It invites them to grow together in holiness and character. Through the trials and joys they face, a good marriage becomes a spiritual process. It fosters mutual growth that nurtures their souls and strengthens their bond. In this light, marriage is a divine calling. It is a journey toward Christlikeness that enriches the couple and everyone they touch.

MARRIAGE IS A COVENANT, NOT A CONTRACT

A critical difference in understanding marriage is seeing it as a covenant rather than a contract. This difference significantly impacts how couples perceive their relationship. A contract depends on specific conditions and mutual obligations. On the other hand, a covenant is an unconditional promise based on mutual devotion and faithfulness. If one person breaches a contract, the other is no longer obligated to continue. However, from a biblical perspective, a covenant endures through difficulties because it represents a higher spiritual commitment.

The Bible describes marriage as a sacred covenant. Malachi 2:14 references a divine covenant between spouses: "The Lord is a witness between you and the wife of your youth...she is your companion and your wife by covenant." This emphasizes that marriage extends beyond personal convenience or emotional comfort. It signifies a profound spiritual union ordained by God Himself. The partners' vows to each other form the core of this marital covenant. These vows are not just ceremonial words or casual promises; they represent a lifelong commitment of unconditional love, fidelity, respect, and mutual support. Marital commitments reflect Christlike virtues such as grace, humility, patience, forgiveness, and self-sacrifice.

In Ephesians 5:25-28, Paul offers a compelling example of this covenantal relationship, urging husbands to love their wives sacrificially, "as Christ loved the church and gave himself up for her." This selfless, sacrificial devotion underscores the seriousness of a marital covenant, where the husband's love mirrors Christ's profound sacrifice and unwavering faithfulness toward humanity. Likewise, wives are called to respect their husbands

(Ephesians 5:33). Respect here is not submission rooted in feelings of inferiority or weakness but rather an expression of trust in God's intentional design for marriage. This mutual exchange of love and respect fosters an environment of harmony, cooperation, and spiritual growth, creating a strong, complementary partnership that flourishes according to God's design.

In contemporary culture, marriage often suffers from a contractual mindset, which easily justifies separation and divorce when expectations are not met or conflicts emerge. By contrast, viewing marriage as a sacred covenant shifts the couple's perspective toward permanence, unconditional commitment, and spiritual perseverance. Instead of being signals to leave, challenges become opportunities to deepen intimacy, foster spiritual growth, and practice forgiveness and grace. As discussed earlier, a covenantal view of marriage does not recognize exit strategies or "Plan B." Instead, couples actively address issues, focusing on healing and growth rather than separation or escape. Such a steadfast commitment honors God, strengthens emotional intimacy, and builds relational resilience.

In sum, a marriage based on covenant rather than contract is characterized by steadfastness, unconditional love, and spiritual integrity. By adopting this covenantal view, couples can fully realize God's intended purpose for marriage, reflecting His divine love and unity in their lifelong partnership.

CHAPTER 2

BUILDING A STRONG FOUNDATION

S hared values and goals are the cornerstone of a strong marital foundation. Just as a house needs a solid foundation to withstand storms, a marriage depends on these shared principles to endure life's inevitable challenges. This chapter explores how couples can build this sturdy foundation by openly sharing their values and goals, cultivating genuine respect for one another, and applying practical biblical teachings. It also highlights the importance of understanding your spouse's personality, needs, and preferences, which are essential elements that foster deeper connection and harmony.

A robust marital foundation is not a one-time achievement, but a dynamic entity that requires ongoing nurturing and deliberate effort. It ensures that both partners are aligned in their vision and aspirations, empowering them to navigate differences and obstacles with unity and grace. Jesus' words in Matthew 7:24-25 vividly illustrate this principle, comparing the wise man to someone who builds his house on the rock, a structure that can stand firm against the winds and floods of life. Similarly, a marriage rooted in shared values, mutual understanding, and a dedicated commitment to God's design can weather any storm.

However, in today's fast-paced and often divided world, many couples struggle to establish or maintain this essential foundation. Disparities in values, unaligned goals, or a lack of understanding can threaten the stability of even the most promising relationships. Nonetheless, with intentional effort and reliance on divine guidance, couples can strengthen their bond and build a resilient marriage that endures through all of life's seasons.

SHARED VALUES AND GOALS

Values are the deeply held beliefs that define what is important to you as individuals and as a couple. These may include faith, honesty, generosity, integrity, family, and service to others. Shared values and goals serve as the guiding principles and aspirations that shape your decisions, priorities, and actions as a couple. They provide a sense of purpose and direction, ensuring that both partners work toward a shared vision.

When both partners share similar values, it creates a sense of unity and purpose, bringing joy and reducing the likelihood of conflict over significant decisions. This shared joy and unity can be a source of hope and inspiration in your marriage journey. Dr. John Gottman, a renowned relationship researcher, emphasizes that shared values play a significant role in contributing to marital satisfaction and stability. Couples who align their core beliefs are better equipped to navigate disagreements and make decisions that honor their relationship (*The Seven Principles for Making Marriage Work*, 1999).

THE ROLE OF SHARED GOALS

Shared goals serve as the foundation for building a strong, meaningful relationship. They can encompass various aspects of life, such as striving for financial stability, nurturing spiritual growth, raising children in a godly home, or achieving critical career milestones. At the core are shared values that guide these aspirations; faith, for example, might inspire both partners to attend church regularly or pray daily, reinforcing their spiritual connection. Similarly, valuing family can lead to intentional efforts to prioritize quality family time and plan memorable vacations together. When couples align on these shared goals and values, they create a bond rooted in mutual purpose, passion, and commitment, fueling a partnership that not only sustains but also enriches their lives.

Practical Applications

Regularly Revisit Your Values: Discuss your individual and shared values. If faith is a shared value, commit to praying together daily or attending church regularly.

Set Short-Term and Long-Term Goals: Break your goals into manageable timeframes. A short-term goal could be attending a marriage seminar, while a long-term goal might be saving for your children's education.

Create a Vision Statement: Write a joint vision statement encapsulating your values and goals as a couple. Example: *"We commit to prioritizing faith, family, and generosity in all aspects of our lives."*

Amos 3:3 asks, *"Can two walk together unless they are agreed?" A shared commitment to values and goals ensures that both partners move in the same direction, fostering harmony and reducing unnecessary conflicts."*

HOW TO FOSTER MUTUAL RESPECT AND UNDERSTANDING IN RELATIONSHIPS

MUTUAL RESPECT

Mutual respect serves as the essential foundation for any healthy and enduring relationship. It involves genuinely honoring each partner's individuality. It also appreciates the unique qualities they bring into the relationship. By actively listening with an open heart and mind, free from judgment or criticism, you create a space where both partners feel genuinely valued and respected. This space empowers them to express themselves authentically. This atmosphere of mutual respect nurtures trust and deepens intimacy. It also fosters a sense of confidence and security. When respect thrives, it ignites a shared strength that empowers couples to face life's challenges together with courage and unity.

MUTUAL UNDERSTANDING

Building a profound understanding of your partner goes far beyond surface-level knowledge; it requires a heartfelt exploration of their needs, passions, and personality. Cultivating this deep awareness enriches emotional intimacy. This awareness equips couples with the empathy needed to navigate conflicts gracefully. Investing time and genuine effort into truly understanding one another lays a resilient foundation, one that supports growth, resilience, and a vibrant, loving connection. As mutual understanding deepens, the relationship blossoms into something truly special. It blossoms into a bond that is alive with love, compassion, and mutual respect.

•   •   •

Practical Applications

Active Listening: Practice fully engaging with your spouse when they speak. This means avoiding distractions, maintaining eye contact, and reflecting on what they say before responding. For example, instead of offering a solution immediately, say, "I hear you're feeling overwhelmed. How can I support you?"

Learn the Basics About Your Spouse: Take time to explore your spouse's complex inner world by discovering their unique love language, as explained in Gary Chapman's insightful book, The 5 Love Languages (1995). Also, consider their personality type and the specific triggers that cause stress in their lives. For example, if your spouse values words of affirmation highly, make it a habit to regularly express your appreciation and encouragement in thoughtful, heartfelt ways. Understanding their love language gives you valuable insights and tools to nurture and strengthen your relationship, fostering a deeper emotional connection and building resilience.

Express Gratitude: Make it a habit to frequently acknowledge your spouse's efforts and contributions, regardless of their size. A simple, sincere "Thank you for taking care of the groceries today" can create a strong sense of appreciation and validation. To enhance this, consider leaving love notes in unexpected places, giving verbal affirmations that highlight their importance to you, or performing thoughtful acts of service that show your genuine care. These gestures cultivate a warm atmosphere of gratitude and deepen your bond, making each partner feel cherished and valued.

Clarify Assumptions: In moments of uncertainty within a relationship, seeking clarity from your spouse is often most beneficial rather than jumping to conclusions about their intentions or emotions. For instance, instead of saying, "You never listen to me," try approaching the conversation with a more constructive and caring tone. You might say, "I feel like there are times when we struggle to communicate, especially during stressful situations. Can we discuss how we can improve our communication during those moments?" This approach opens the door to an honest dialogue. It also fosters an in-depth understanding between partners.

The wisdom found in Philippians 2:3-4 serves as an essential guide in these discussions, advising us to value others above ourselves, not focusing solely on our interests, but on the interests of others. This perspective encourages us to adopt a mindset of humility and empathy, which is vital for nurturing a harmonious relationship. By genuinely prioritizing your spouse's feelings and perspectives, you are actively working to create an environment built on mutual respect, trust, and emotional safety. Such a commitment can significantly enhance the depth and resilience of your relationship, leading to a partnership where both individuals feel valued and understood.

THE THREE FOUNDATION PRINCIPLES OF MARRIAGE: LOVE, RESPECT, AND SUBMISSION

Love as the Foundation of God-Honoring Marriage

Husbands are called to embody a profound and sacrificial love for their wives, mirroring the love that Christ has for the church, as illustrated in Ephesians 5:25. This type of love transcends mere affection; it is a commitment that places the well-being, happiness, and personal growth of the wife above the husband's interests. It is a selfless devotion that may compel a husband to make significant sacrifices, even to the point of laying down his own life for her if necessary.

This love goes beyond acts of kindness or romantic

gestures; it is a daily choice to prioritize her needs and nurture her spirit and talents. The essence of this calling is rooted in the understanding that a husband has made a conscious choice to commit to his wife. Thus, he must love her with the depth and intensity that he would give to his own life. In this context, true love is not merely a feeling but an active expression of commitment, respect, and responsibility toward the partnership they have chosen to build together.

Respect as the Framework of God-Honoring Marriage

As Scripture profoundly declares in Ephesians 5:33, *"Let each one of you love his wife as himself, and let the wife see that she respects her husband."* This divine instruction is not a cultural suggestion; it is a covenantal principle. Respect is not merely about manners or protocol; it is the very atmosphere in which a godly man breathes and thrives. It affirms his role as the spiritual head of the home, not as a tyrant but as a servant-leader under Christ.

To respect your husband is to honor the weight he carries, the silent burdens, the daily decisions, the relentless pursuit to provide, protect, and lead. It means esteeming his contributions, both visible and unseen. It means choosing, with intentionality, to speak life into his spirit through affirming words, thoughtful gestures, and consistent emotional support. Whether through being his confidant, cheering his progress, or offering grace in moments of failure, your respect becomes his refuge.

Respect also means active submission, not passivity, but purposeful alignment with God's order. Just as husbands are commanded to love sacrificially, *even to the point of laying down their lives* (Ephesians 5:25), wives are called to submit *as unto the Lord* (Ephesians 5:22). This submission is not blind compli-

ance; it is a willful yielding to his God-ordained leadership,
provided it does not violate the Lord's commands. You honor
his leadership not because he is flawless, but because God has
entrusted it to him. Your trust is not in his perfection, but in
God's providence.

Marriage is not a democracy; it is a divine design. When
you, as a wife, respect your husband even in disagreement, you
are not only building him; you are building the covenant.
Through open dialogue, gentleness in correction, and a heart
that leans toward unity, you become a builder of your house
(Proverbs 14:1), anchoring your marriage in Christ-centered
strength.

Submission as a Sacred Partnership

Many misunderstand submission as surrendering power,
but biblically, submission is a partnership, a beautiful, powerful
alignment under God's authority. As Ephesians 5:21 declares,
"Submit to one another out of reverence for Christ." This mutual
submission is not a tug-of-war, but a mutual laying down of
ego in favor of shared purpose. It is the soil where grace grows
and where both husband and wife flourish.

Submission is not about one ruling and the other yielding;
it is about both prioritizing each other's needs above their own,
modeling the selfless love of Christ. The husband, submitting
to Christ's example, lays down his life. The wife, in turn,
submits with trust, knowing she is safeguarded by his love and
shielded by his leadership. Together, they mirror the relationship between Christ and the Church, a dynamic exchange of
love, sacrifice, and reverence.

When a couple submits to God first, their marriage
becomes a living testimony to God's love. They invite His
wisdom into their decisions, His Spirit into their communica-

tion, and His peace into their storms. This type of marriage is not merely functional; it is fruitful. It becomes a sanctuary where grace is practiced daily, and growth is inevitable.

Such mutual submission cultivates an environment where both partners can thrive individually and together. It encourages spiritual maturity, emotional safety, and a deep sense of unity that transcends hardship. In this sacred exchange, submission is no longer a burden; it becomes a blessing. It is no longer a duty; it becomes a delight, born from a deep desire to walk in God's perfect design for love, leadership, and legacy.

PRACTICAL APPLICATIONS

A Christ-centered marriage is not built merely on feelings—it is forged through deliberate actions that reflect love, respect, and submission to God's divine order. As James 1:22 reminds us, *"Do not merely listen to the word, and so deceive yourselves. Do what it says."* The beauty of marriage blossoms when biblical truth is not only believed but lived out daily through practical, Spirit-led choices.

Husbands: Lead with love through action and presence. As Ephesians 5:25 commands, *"Husbands, love your wives, just as Christ loved the church and gave himself up for her."* Your leadership begins with sacrificial love, not dominion. Express this love through thoughtful and tangible acts that convey care, attentiveness, and delight in your wife. Surprise her with a warm, comforting meal after a long, exhausting day. You can also step in to manage household responsibilities she usually handles, such as doing the dishes, folding laundry, or supervising the children. These actions demonstrate that her well-being is your joy and responsibility.

Listen with intentionality. Not to solve or fix, but to understand. Offer your full attention as she shares her heart. Remove distractions, silence judgment, and lean in, so she knows her voice is not only heard but cherished. Create sacred spaces of emotional safety, whether it's a cozy corner in your home, a peaceful stroll together, or uninterrupted time on the couch. Let these moments become sanctuaries where she feels free to speak her truth without fear. When you foster emotional safety, you are nurturing intimacy, trust, and unity in the very soil God designed for your covenant to thrive.

Wives: Reflect respect through honor and encouragement. As Ephesians 5:33 instructs, *"The wife must respect her husband."* This respect is not passive; it is powerful. It is the oxygen that fuels a man's confidence and calling. When you honor your husband, you elevate the man God has called him to be. Recognize and appreciate his tireless efforts in his work, in your home, and his personal growth. Celebrate his strengths publicly and privately. When correction is needed, let your feedback be wrapped in gentleness, clarity, and grace, offering warmth rather than wounds.

Support his role as the spiritual leader of your home. This doesn't mean agreeing with everything blindly, but choosing to stand with him, even when life's pressures weigh heavily on his shoulders. Speak life into his leadership. Let him know you believe in the vision God has placed in his heart. Engage in deep, meaningful conversations that affirm his decisions, hopes, and dreams. Invite collaboration and work toward shared goals that foster unity and purpose. Your respect doesn't make you less; it makes your marriage more. It is your spiritual strength on display—nurturing a home rooted in biblical order and divine love.

Both: Build on the rock through prayer and God's Word. A marriage that endures kneels together before God. As Ecclesiastes 4:12 says, *"A cord of three strands is not quickly broken."* Prioritize time to pray together, bringing your praises, petitions, and pains before the Lord. Let Scripture be your compass. Study God's Word as a couple, allowing His truth to guide your decisions and strengthen your bond.

Above all, submit to Christ as the ultimate authority in your marriage. When both husband and wife yield to Him, your relationship is not only sustained, it is sanctified. In Christ, you will find wisdom for every challenge, peace in every storm, and joy in every season.

Activity: Values and Goals Alignment Exercise

Step 1: Individual Reflection: Write down your top five values and personal goals. Reflect on how these align with God's Word and your priorities in relationships.
Step 2: Discuss Your Values and Goals with Your Spouse: Share your values and goals with your spouse. Are there areas where you need to align more closely?
Step 3: Action Plan: Create a list of shared values and goals. Commit to revisiting this list regularly and adjusting as needed.

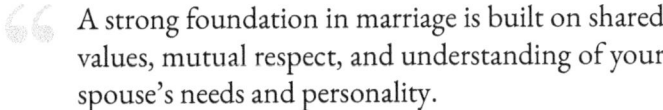

A strong foundation in marriage is built on shared values, mutual respect, and understanding of your spouse's needs and personality.

Aligning your relationship with biblical principles and encouraging open communication can help you build a marriage that honors God and flourishes through life's challenges.

CHAPTER 3

RELATIONSHIP MAINTENANCE

A COVENANT WORTH TENDING

A thriving marriage does not happen by chance; it is the fruit of consistent, intentional investment. Just as the military conducts preventive maintenance to keep vital equipment mission-ready, so too must couples engage in relational maintenance to keep their covenant strong and enduring. This sacred commitment to nurture, realign, and strengthen the marital bond is not a one-time effort but a continual act of stewardship. Hebrews 13:4 declares, *"Marriage should be honored by all, and the marriage bed kept pure."* To honor marriage is to tend to it, to give it care before there is a crisis, and attention before there is erosion. Regular check-ins, emotional, spiritual, and practical- allow couples to assess their connection, adjust course when needed, and maintain unity in a world that pulls relationships apart.

DAILY ACTS OF LOVE AND SERVICE

Relationship maintenance begins in the small, often unseen, acts of love. Preparing your spouse's favorite meal, offering a listening ear after a long day, or sharing in household responsibilities are not merely chores; they are ministries of grace. As Galatians 5:13 exhorts, *"Serve one another humbly in love."* These gestures act as oil to the gears of marriage, preventing the friction of unmet expectations and unspoken frustrations from causing larger breakdowns.

When minor offenses are ignored, they build up like rust over time, leading to emotional distance and dissatisfaction. However, couples who handle these little issues with honesty and grace can prevent severe damage and nurture a resilient love through every season. Ignoring minor problems only allows them to grow into larger issues. Through attention, prayer, and action, couples can restore unity and uphold the marriage's sacredness.

BIBLICAL PILLARS OF RELATIONSHIP MAINTENANCE

Regular Communication

Communication is more than exchanging information. It is the practice of uncovering what is hidden in the heart. Ephesians 4:29 says, *"Do not let any unwholesome talk come out of your mouths, but only what helps build others up."* Words should strengthen, not hurt—tone matters. Timing matters. Listening matters.

Speak the truth, but do it with grace. Share burdens, but stay mindful of each other's capacity. Ask questions that invite honesty. Do not interrupt. Avoid assuming motives. Listen with the desire to understand, not to defend. When communication is healthy, the relationship remains open, humble, and safe. When a couple stops communicating regularly, they stop growing. Silence creates space for distance. Words bridge that distance. Make time daily to connect. Speak life into one another. Let communication become your altar, where trust is rebuilt continually.

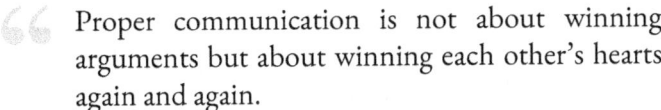

> Proper communication is not about winning arguments but about winning each other's hearts again and again.

Conflict Resolution

Conflict is not the enemy. Avoidance is a great enemy. Romans 12:18 reminds us, *"If it is possible, as far as it depends on you, live at peace with everyone."* Peace does not come from ignoring issues, but from confronting them with humility and purpose. Learn how to approach your spouse without provoking them. Use gentle words. Do not raise your voice to prove a point. Do not rehearse your anger before addressing the concern. Pray before speaking. Let God purify your heart first. Deal with issues while they are small. Apologize quickly. Forgive fully.

Refuse to allow resentment to build. Bitterness poisons affection. Unresolved offense opens the door to isolation. Choose reconciliation over pride. The goal is not to win arguments but to win each other back. Keep short accounts. Extend mercy. Let every conflict end in restoration.

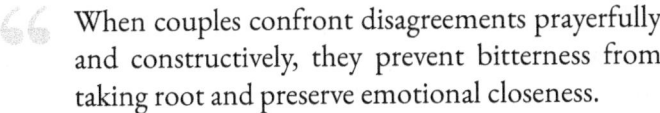

> When couples confront disagreements prayerfully and constructively, they prevent bitterness from taking root and preserve emotional closeness.

Intimacy Formation

Intimacy does not appear automatically. It must be cultivated. Genesis 2:25 declares, *"Adam and his wife were both naked, and they felt no shame.*" This reveals God's design, openness without fear. Emotional intimacy requires vulnerability. Physical intimacy involves trust. Spiritual intimacy requires unity of purpose. Emotional intimacy develops when couples are open and honest about their fears, disappointments, and desires. Do not hide. Speak truthfully. Share dreams and struggles. Let yourself be seen. Make time to discuss topics beyond surface-level issues.

Physical intimacy is sacred. It is not a reward for good behavior. It is a gift God gives to strengthen the marriage bond. Do not withhold affection out of spite. Do not neglect physical closeness because of busyness. Keep your connection alive. Prioritize touch, kindness, and shared moments of closeness. Spiritual intimacy deepens when couples pray together, worship together, and submit together to God's Word. This type of intimacy binds the marriage with a purpose that transcends circumstances.

 Couples must nurture intimacy as a holy priority, not an optional extra.

Spiritual Growth and Shared Purpose

Unless the Lord builds the house, the builders labor in vain (Psalm 127:1). A marriage not rooted in Christ cannot stand firm. The spiritual health of a couple determines the strength of their partnership. Spiritual growth requires more than church attendance. It requires personal surrender. Husbands must lead their homes in truth. Wives must encourage and support that leadership. Both must walk in humility before God.

Pray together daily. Read Scripture aloud. Engage in a biblical fast when major decisions require careful consideration. Speak blessings over one another. Ask God for direction. Invite

Him into every part of your marriage. Shared purpose gives your marriage a sense of purpose. When both partners live for God's glory, their love grows deeper. Their decisions carry eternal weight. Their unity becomes unbreakable. Do not treat spiritual growth as optional. It is the foundation. Without it, the structure weakens. With it, every part of your marriage thrives.

Always remember this: spiritual alignment is more than shared faith; it is about walking the journey side by side, yoked together in Christ. This shared pursuit gives the marriage a mission, a direction, and a holy resilience that can endure hardship and celebrate triumph with eternal perspective.

Exhortation

Relationship maintenance is not a chore. It is a sacred duty. It reflects obedience to God's command and reverence for the gift of marriage. Colossians 3:14 reminds us, *"Above all these put on love, which binds everything together in perfect harmony."* Invest daily. Speak gently. Forgive quickly. Pursue intimacy. Walk with God. Your marriage is not just a personal covenant; it is a living testimony of Christ's love for His Church.

Proactive Marital Investment

Proactive marital investment involves purposeful relationship-building activities even when no issues are apparent. Just as you wouldn't wait for a vehicle to break down before doing preventive maintenance, couples should actively nurture their relationship. Research consistently shows that couples who invest proactively in their relationship experience greater satisfaction, deeper emotional intimacy, and increased resilience in facing challenges (McNulty, 2019). Preventive maintenance in marriage offers several key benefits:

i. **Reduced Conflict Likelihood:** Consistent, proactive communication helps prevent misunderstandings and conflicts, creating a more peaceful relationship environment.
ii. **Enhanced Intimacy:** Intentional acts of kindness, regular date nights, and shared activities nurture emotional and physical closeness.
iii. **Greater Commitment and Resilience:** Participating in joint activities and shared spiritual growth strengthens couples' commitment and helps them handle inevitable difficulties.
iv. **Deeper Spiritual Connection:** Aligning a marriage with biblical principles fosters spiritual intimacy, cultivating mutual support and understanding.

UNDERSTANDING AND MAINTAINING ROLES IN MARRIAGE

The Word of God provides a clear and purposeful design for the roles of husbands and wives. These roles are not rooted in culture, preference, or personal opinion—they are rooted in divine intention. As stated in Ephesians 5:22-25, wives are called to submit to their husbands *as to the Lord*, and husbands are commanded to love their wives *as Christ loved the Church and gave Himself up for her*. These distinct roles are not intended to create a hierarchy of value, but to cultivate harmony, order, and unity under God's authority.

God did not create confusion. He created complementarity, where each role contributes uniquely to the strength and balance of the whole. The husband's leadership is sacrificial and servant-hearted. The wife's submission is one of trust and honor. Both are accountable to Christ. Together, they reflect the mystery of Christ and His Church. In today's world, these roles are often misunderstood or rejected. Cultural narratives push against biblical order. Society promotes role reversals, power struggles, and individual autonomy above covenant faithfulness. These influences sow division where God intends unity. The result is not freedom but conflict, confusion, and emotional disconnection within marriages.

Many couples struggle not because of a lack of love, but because they are attempting to live out marriage on the world's terms rather than God's truth. When biblical roles are dismissed or distorted, the relationship loses its foundation. Authority becomes abuse. Submission becomes silence. Love becomes performance. Respect becomes optional.

To build a healthy marriage, couples must return to the Scriptures. They must be willing to differentiate between biblical instruction and cultural opinion. God's Word is not outdated; it is eternal. His design for marriage is not restrictive; it is redemptive. When husbands embrace their calling to lead with humility, and wives respond with respect and trust, the marriage becomes a testimony of God's wisdom.

This alignment produces peace, stability, and spiritual strength. It does not enslave; it sets the marriage free to function as it was designed. Let us not be shaped by culture, but transformed by the renewing of our minds (Romans 12:2). Let us honor the roles God has given, knowing that they are not about superiority, but about faithfulness to God's order and obedience to His will.

BIBLICAL ROLES: LEADERSHIP AND SUPPORT

The husband's role is not founded on power but on love. Scripture teaches that the husband is to lead his home as Christ leads the Church, with sacrifice, not selfishness. *"Husbands, love your wives, just as Christ loved the church and gave himself up for her"* (Ephesians 5:25). Christ did not dominate the Church. He died for her. He bore her burdens. He served her for her good. A husband's leadership must follow this same path.

He is called to lead spiritually by anchoring his family in the Word of God. He must set the tone for prayer, worship, and righteous living. He leads emotionally by creating a safe space where his wife feels seen and valued. He leads practically by taking initiative in decision-making while listening and seeking the counsel of his wife, who stands beside him, not behind him. His leadership is measured by humility, not control.

The wife's role is not secondary but essential. Genesis 2:18 describes her as a "helper," using the Hebrew word *ezer*, a word also used to describe God's help to Israel. This is not a position of inferiority. It is a position of strength, wisdom, and deep value. The wife is divinely appointed to support, strengthen, and stabilize the marriage through her presence, discernment, and godly influence.

By encouraging her husband's leadership, the wife contributes to the unity of the home. She does not lose her voice; she amplifies the covenant through her words, her counsel, and her example. A wife who embraces her God-given role nurtures peace in her home. She deepens emotional intimacy through trust. She guards the heart of her husband with prayer and wisdom. She serves not out of obligation, but out of an understanding that her role is sacred.

The foundation of these roles is mutual submission to Christ (Ephesians 5:21). Neither spouse exists to exalt self. Each yields to Christ as the ultimate head. Submission to one another is not about one ruling and the other following blindly. It is about choosing to honor one another's roles with reverence for God's design. It is about trust, not territory. It is about service, not status.

DISTORTIONS AND MISCONCEPTIONS

When society rejects God's order, confusion follows. Cultural trends often swing between extremes, either depicting marriage as an outdated control system or redefining roles into pointless preferences. These distortions are not merely ideological; they impact genuine relationships, daily routines, and expectations in marriage. Feminist ideologies, while advocating for justice and female dignity, have sometimes misinterpreted biblical submission as weakness or slavery. However, true submission is not passive; it is an active choice to embody Christ's humility and order. As Scripture teaches, submission is not about silence or surrendering intellect but about trusting God's design for growth and flourishing.

Masculinist perspectives often go to the opposite extreme, confusing biblical leadership with dominance. Some men interpret their role as permission to control rather than to serve. They demand authority without embracing the responsibility that comes with it. This is not leadership; it is distortion. Scripture calls for leadership that dies to self daily.

Media and pop culture deepen this confusion. Marriages are portrayed as battlegrounds for control. Spouses are seen as competitors rather than covenant partners. Popular voices promote independence without interdependence, encouraging couples to prioritize personal rights over shared responsibilities.

These misconceptions shape behavior. A man may neglect his spiritual leadership out of fear of being labeled controlling.

A woman may suppress her gifts out of fear she will overstep. Couples drift into isolation, misunderstanding one another's intentions and resisting the roles designed to bring them together.

PRACTICAL MISAPPLICATIONS IN EVERYDAY LIFE

These distortions do not remain theoretical. They seep into daily choices, tone, and expectations. For example:

  i. A husband may believe he must control every decision, leaving no room for his wife's wisdom or input.
  ii. A wife may feel compelled to suppress her calling or dreams, believing submission means silence.
  iii. Couples may avoid healthy dependence, fearing that honoring biblical roles will limit their potential.

These subtle misconceptions influence how spouses perceive each other. They diminish the relationship to a negotiation instead of a sacred bond. Over time, this change leads to emotional disconnection and spiritual misalignment. To restore the marriage, couples must recognize these distortions, reject them, and return to the truth of Scripture. Biblical roles are not chains; they are channels through which grace flows. They are not about what each spouse gains, but about how each serves, supports, and sacrifices under the lordship of Christ.

THE SUBTLE INFLUENCE OF CULTURAL NARRATIVES

Cultural narratives carry power—not only in what they say, but in what they subtly normalize. Over time, these influences shape expectations, priorities, and definitions of identity. When absorbed uncritically, they can distort the biblical design for marriage, replacing God's truth with human-manufactured ideals that fragment instead of unify. One of the greatest threats to marital health today is not blatant rebellion against Scripture, but the slow drift toward cultural philosophies that redefine roles without regard for God's order.

The Independent Woman Narrative: This message teaches women that fulfillment comes through absolute self-reliance. Independence is elevated above relationships. Dependence is portrayed as a loss of dignity. Submission is viewed as a weakness or regression. While strength, competence, and initiative are God-given traits, marriage is not designed to be a competition for autonomy.

Biblical marriage thrives on mutual dependence. Scripture does not erase a woman's agency. It invites her to use her strength to build up her husband, her household, and her legacy. As Proverbs 31 shows, a godly woman is not idle; she is industrious, wise, and respected. Yet her strength flows through her support of God's design, not opposition to it.

The Dominant Male Narrative: This mindset falsely equates leadership with control. It misuses Scripture to justify the wife's silence and unchecked authority for the husband. It distorts the model Christ gave, where headship is grounded in self-denial, not self-promotion. Authentic biblical leadership reflects Christ's example: sacrificial, patient, and protective. It does not crush. It covers. It does not demand submission. It wins it through service. When a husband exercises leadership apart from humility, the home becomes a battlefield rather than a refuge.

WHY THESE DISTORTIONS PERSIST

Several factors contribute to the persistence of these distorted views. Cultural shifts prioritize self-interest over sacrifice. Feminist ideologies, while historically necessary in correcting injustices, sometimes present biblical submission as outdated or oppressive. Masculinist ideologies counter with authoritarianism, often masked as biblical headship.

As Dr. Carrie Miles explains in *The Redemption of Love* (2006), changes in the economic structure and the rise of individualism have reshaped how people view marriage and gender. Media portrayals often reinforce power struggles rather than cooperation, glamorizing conflict and diminishing biblical roles as obsolete. Rather than rejecting roles or clinging to harmful distortions, couples must return to God's Word.

Scripture does not confuse submission with silence, nor does it equate leadership with superiority. It presents a relationship of mutual strength, guided by divine design and sustained by grace. Timothy Keller wrote in *The Meaning of Marriage* (2011), "When we understand marriage as a reflection of the gospel, we see the beauty of roles as an opportunity to serve and love one another." This is the heart of biblical complementarity, not hierarchy, but holiness.

RESTORING THE KINGDOM PATTERN

A marriage that honors God resists cultural drift by anchoring itself in Scripture. It does not adjust roles to match societal trends. It realigns hearts with truth. It establishes a covenant shaped not by trends but by timeless principles.

1. Complementarity over Competition: God created man and woman to reflect His image in distinct but unified ways. Differences in role are not flaws. They are the foundation for unity. When spouses recognize their unique callings and live them with humility, the result is balance and peace. The marriage becomes a testimony of cooperation, not comparison. Each partner brings what the other does not. This is not an imbalance; it is design. When each role is embraced, the relationship becomes stronger, more fruitful, and more secure.

2. Joint Submission to Christ: Mutual submission is the anchor of all biblical roles (Ephesians 5:21). When both husband and wife place Christ as Lord over their home, decision-making is filtered through His Word. Personal agendas are surrendered. Conflicts are resolved with humility. Authority is exercised in fear of God. This shared submission cultivates unity and clarity amid confusion.

3. Intentional Commitment to Biblical Roles: Living out biblical roles is not accidental. It requires discipline, prayer, and conviction. Husbands must lead with consistency, patience, and spiritual covering. Wives must support with strength, trust, and wisdom. This requires daily surrender, not occasional effort. When these roles are walked out with love and integrity, they create an environment where grace flows, respect grows, and love is sustained. The home becomes a lighthouse to a confused world.

THE BEAUTY OF COMPLEMENTARITY

Biblical roles are not about worth; they are about function. God did not design one to be more critical. He created each to contribute to a greater whole. When rightly understood, complementarity showcases the Gospel. Christ leads. The Church responds. Both display God's glory in different ways.

1. Leadership as Service: True leadership is not control. It is a sacrifice. Christ laid down His life for the Church. Husbands must do the same. This kind of leadership is not passive. It initiates. It prays. It protects. It listens. It corrects in love.

Example: A husband who senses his wife's emotional fatigue and chooses to lead her in prayer, offer encouragement, and take on a greater share of the household responsibilities reflects the heart of Christ.

2. Help as Strength: Help is not weakness. *Ezer* is the same word used for God as our helper in times of trouble. It speaks of essential presence, vital wisdom, and sustaining strength. A wife who walks in her calling supports not by shrinking but by stabilizing.

Example: A wife who manages the family's finances with discernment, prepares the home for seasons ahead, and speaks wisdom into family decisions fulfills her God-given role.

Practical Reflection

Consider where cultural ideas have shaped your expectations more than God's truth. Reflect on how your strengths uniquely contribute to your marriage. Are you leading with humility? Are you supporting with strength?

PRACTICAL APPLICATIONS FOR BIBLICAL LEADERSHIP

God's design for the husband's role in marriage is patterned after Christ's leadership over the Church, marked by sacrifice, service, wisdom, and love. Authentic leadership is not passive, selfish, or controlling. It is humble, active, and deeply rooted in a desire to honor God while strengthening the marriage covenant. As Ephesians 5:25 teaches, *"Husbands, love your wives, just as Christ loved the church and gave himself up for her."*

1. Spiritual Leadership

What It Looks Like: The husband leads the home in spiritual disciplines. He sets the tone for prayer, Scripture engagement, worship, and godly decision-making. He initiates spiritual growth, both personally and corporately.

Example: A husband might lead a family in a Bible reading plan or guide a devotional time after dinner. He may lead in prayer during moments of family crisis or help resolve conflict with grace, always considering his wife's voice. Planning family activities that uphold Christ-centered values is another way to reflect spiritual leadership.

2. Emotional Leadership

What It Looks Like: The husband creates a safe and attentive space where his wife can share her burdens. He does not dismiss her feelings or rush to fix everything. He listens with humility and provides assurance through his presence.

Example: When his wife feels overwhelmed or discouraged, a husband listens patiently, prays with her, and provides gentle encouragement. He remains emotionally steady and available, modeling the comfort of Christ.

3. Physical Leadership (Protection)

What It Looks Like: The husband takes responsibility for the physical well-being of his household. He ensures the safety and order of the environment, using discretion to guard against both internal and external threats.

Example: A husband handles issues like home repairs, family safety plans, or routine security checks. He takes initiative in addressing problems and creates an atmosphere of stability.

4. Provision
What It Looks Like: The husband works diligently to provide for his family's material needs. He handles finances with integrity, plans, and resists impulsivity.

Example: A husband creates a family budget that aligns with shared goals. He seeks ways to steward resources wisely, prioritizing needs, avoiding unnecessary debt, and involving his wife in financial decisions.

PRACTICAL APPLICATIONS FOR BIBLICAL HELP

The role of the wife, as described in **Genesis 2:18**, is to be a "helper"—a term that reflects strength, wisdom, and divine purpose. The Hebrew word *ezer* signifies vital support, the same term used to describe God as our Helper. A godly wife strengthens her husband's leadership and enriches the marriage through active, Spirit-led engagement.

1. Supportive Leadership
What It Looks Like: The wife stands beside her husband as a trusted encourager. She strengthens his leadership by offering insight, perspective, and accountability. Her support is intentional, not passive.

Example: A wife may offer wise counsel before a significant decision, helping her husband see factors he may not have considered. She provides honest and respectful feedback that guides and confirms his role.

2. Adviser Role
What It Looks Like: The wife serves as her husband's primary sounding board. She offers discernment and clarity, helping him process ideas, challenges, and choices with wisdom and balance.

Example: A wife may help her husband navigate a job opportunity by discussing spiritual, emotional, and practical implications. Her perspective helps bring peace and direction.

3. Managing Sustainment
What It Looks Like: The wife oversees the practical rhythms of the home. She organizes, coordinates, and maintains systems that sustain the family's stability.

Example: A wife creates a monthly budget, tracks spending, and plans grocery shopping around nutritional and financial needs. Her planning promotes peace and stewardship within the home.

4. Nurturing Atmosphere
What It Looks Like: The wife fosters warmth, unity, and emotional strength within the home. She cultivates habits and rhythms that build joy, connection, and peace.

Example: A wife plans family dinners, creates intentional bonding activities, and facilitates conversations that deepen relationships. Her presence turns the home into a place of restoration.

ACTIVITY

Reclaiming Roles in Your Marriage

Step 1: Reflect on Distortions: Write down any cultural beliefs, media messages, or misconceptions that may have shaped your understanding of marital roles. Identify any areas where worldly values have replaced biblical truth.

Step 2: Revisit Scripture Together: Read and discuss Ephesians 5:22-33 and Genesis 2:18. Reflect on how these passages define the roles of husbands and wives. Talk about what parts resonate, challenge, or convict you.

Step 3: Commit to Growth: Choose one specific action to embody your God-given role this week.

• **Husbands:** Lead prayer or ask how you can support your wife spiritually.

• **Wives:** Offer affirmation and speak life into your husband's leadership.

PRACTICAL EXERCISES

1. Marital Self-Assessment Inventory

• Reflect on key areas: spiritual unity, emotional connection, communication, conflict resolution, and daily responsibilities.

• Write down strengths and areas needing improvement.

• Schedule time with your spouse to discuss and pray over these reflections.

2. Role Reflection Exercise

• **Personal Reflection:** Identify the roles you currently fulfill. Evaluate whether they reflect God's Word or cultural expectations.

• **Couple Discussion:** Share your reflections. Discuss the influence of media, upbringing, and society on your understanding of leadership and help.

• **Action Plan:** Create two or three practical goals to strengthen biblical roles in your marriage. Include a plan for accountability, prayer, and mutual encouragement.

CHAPTER 4
REGULAR RELATIONSHIP CHECK-UPS

Marriage, like the human body, requires care and attention. It cannot be left to autopilot. Scripture reminds us in Song of Solomon 2:15, *"Catch for us the foxes, the little foxes that ruin the vineyards, our vineyards that are in bloom."* The health of a marriage is often compromised not by dramatic failures but by subtle neglect. Minor misunderstandings, unspoken disappointments, and buried frustrations, if unchecked, become the foxes that spoil intimacy.

Relationships were never meant to drift unattended. They must be cultivated through intentional time, ongoing reflection, and open conversation. Regular check-ins provide couples with space to pause, assess, and reconnect. Just as wise stewards examine what has been entrusted to them, so should spouses take time to explore their covenant, its condition, its rhythms, and its fruit.

THE PRINCIPLE OF PREVENTIVE MAINTENANCE

The practice of preventive care is embedded in Scripture and reflected in practical wisdom. Proverbs 27:23 instructs, *"Be sure you know the condition of your flocks, give careful attention to your herds.*" In modern terms, this is a call to stewardship. Whether caring for land, family, or covenant, the principle remains: what is not examined cannot be preserved. In the military, there is a long-standing tradition known as "Motorpool Monday." Every week, soldiers inspect their vehicles and equipment to ensure they are in good working order. They check fluid levels, inspect for wear, and address minor issues before they escalate into breakdowns. This discipline ensures readiness and prolongs functionality.

Relationships need the same kind of attention. Weekly or monthly marital check-ins function as relational motorpools. Couples pause, inspect the state of their communication, examine emotional distance, and address any signs of fatigue or disconnection. This habit prevents problems from becoming patterns. It transforms maintenance into ministry.

PANCAKE SATURDAY

In my own home, we have established a tradition we call "Pancake Saturday." Every week, we gather at the kitchen counter and prepare pancakes as a family. The meal is simple, but the meaning is profound. It has become our sacred space for connection. During this time, we talk about the highs and lows of the week. We listen to each other patiently, without hurrying. Sometimes, we share laughs over memories; other times, we talk about difficulties. The goal isn't perfection, but presence. These gatherings serve as our casual check-ins, grounded in joy, motivated by routine, and filled with spiritual growth.

For example, my children might share something that's been bothering them. My wife and I use this time to realign our expectations, revisit our goals, or enjoy being in the exact moment together. It strengthens our unity. It invites the Holy

Spirit into our rhythm. It gives shape to what Deuteronomy 6:7 describes—*"Talk about them when you sit at home and when you walk along the road..."* Ordinary moments become sacred touchpoints when God is invited in.

SPIRITUAL IMPLICATIONS AND MARITAL IMPACT

Regular relationship check-ins are not just emotional exercises. They are acts of spiritual obedience. **1 Peter 3:7** commands husbands to dwell with their wives with understanding. This requires listening, reflection, and intentional pursuit. A husband who checks in with his wife honors God. A wife who shares her heart with grace builds trust. Together, they guard their unity and protect their covenant. These check-ins bring hidden things to light. They expose tension early. They reveal where encouragement is needed. They help couples course-correct before damage deepens. Over time, they create patterns of grace that fortify the marriage through seasons of growth and strain.

WHY SCHEDULING MATTERS

Scheduling regular relationship check-ins ensures that time is deliberately set aside to focus on the health of the relationship. Without planning, discussions about important topics are often postponed or overlooked amid the busyness of daily life. Dr. Sue Johnson, founder of Emotionally Focused Therapy (EFT), emphasizes the importance of predictable patterns of connection, noting that couples who intentionally engage with each other emotionally are better equipped to handle life's stresses (Hold Me Tight, 2008). Predictability builds trust, allowing both partners to approach conversations with a sense of security and readiness.

Just as the military prioritizes Motorpool Monday to prevent equipment failure, couples can establish a regular check-in tradition to maintain the health of their relationship. Consistency is essential, whether it's every Saturday morning, like my family's Pancake Saturday, or a walk after dinner twice a week. These intentional moments provide opportunities to strengthen bonds, address concerns, and celebrate progress.

STEPS FOR IDENTIFYING AND ADDRESSING MINOR ISSUES

Insignificant issues, when ignored, do not disappear. They settle quietly in the corners of the relationship—collecting dust, growing roots, and building walls. Song of Solomon 2:15 warns us to *"catch for us the foxes, the little foxes that ruin the vineyards..."* These foxes are subtle. They are unmet expectations, recurring frustrations, misunderstood words, and delayed conversations. Left unchecked, they damage the intimacy God designed for marriage.

Regular relationship check-ins provide an intentional and safe setting to expose these issues, not to wound but to heal. These conversations are not for assigning blame or defending positions. They are sacred spaces for mutual growth, transparency, and reconnection under the lordship of Christ.

1. Be Honest Yet Gentle: Truth must be spoken, but it must be clothed in grace. Ephesians 4:15 instructs us to *"speak the truth in love."* This principle safeguards the heart while addressing the issue. It is not enough to be right; the tone and timing of your words must reflect the Spirit of Christ. Avoid accusatory language. Replace blame with vulnerability. "You always..." and "You never..." harden the heart. "I feel..." and "I need..." open it. A gentle tone disarms. A gracious word softens resistance.

Example: Instead of saying, "You never help with the

housework," say, "I've been feeling overwhelmed lately and would appreciate more help with the chores." Instead of saying, "You always forget our anniversary," try saying, "I felt hurt when our anniversary passed without acknowledgment." These statements express need without accusation. They invite empathy rather than defense.

2. Focus on One Issue at a Time: A scattered conversation will yield scattered results. Proverbs 25:11 says, *"A word fitly spoken is like apples of gold in a setting of silver."* Timing and focus matter. Overloading a conversation with too many concerns at once can cause confusion, frustration, or retreat. Choose one concern. Speak to it clearly. Seek understanding before introducing another. Honor the value of each issue by giving it the space and time it deserves.

Example: If emotional distance has grown, stay in that lane. Talk about connection. Avoid veering off into discussions about finances, parenting challenges, or unresolved issues. One focus allows deeper listening and more intentional response. It prevents defensiveness and nurtures clarity.

3. Collaborate on Solutions: Marriage is not a battleground for winning points; it is a covenant rooted in oneness. Ecclesiastes 4:9 declares, *"Two are better than one, because they have a good return for their labor."* When couples shift from confrontation to collaboration, they move from division to unity. Seek solutions together. Ask, "What can we both do differently?" Identify what healing looks like, then walk toward it hand in hand. Unity is strengthened not just by agreement, but by action.

Example: If one spouse feels neglected, agree on a daily routine of undistracted time, whether 30 minutes of conversation or a weekly shared activity. If there's a disconnection, explore something new together. If stress becomes overwhelming, consider simplifying responsibilities together. Let the solution be mutual, not one-sided.

BIBLICAL REFLECTION

These steps are not merely relational wisdom; they are spiritual disciplines. They reflect humility, self-control, gentleness, and mutual submission, all fruits of the Spirit. As Colossians 3:12-14 teaches, *"Clothe yourselves with compassion, kindness, humility, gentleness and patience... and over all these virtues put on love, which binds them all together in perfect unity."*

Unity in marriage is preserved by how small things are handled. A healthy marriage is not conflict-free; it is characterized by quick listening, slow and gentle speaking, and an eagerness to forgive. Addressing measly issues regularly will protect the larger picture of your marriage and honor the covenant you made before God.

ALTERNATIVE OPTIONS FOR QUALITY TIME

Traditional Western concepts, such as "date nights," often fall short in practicality and may not effectively resonate with or align seamlessly with diverse cultural customs and values. For many, the standard dinner-and-a-movie format does not reflect their unique social norms or relationship dynamics. Different cultures may prioritize communal activities, family involvement, or even seasonal celebrations as their primary means of connecting.

Consequently, the rigid expectations of a "date night" may overlook the rich diversity of interpersonal engagement that characterizes various traditions, leading to a disconnect between Western practices and those of other cultures. Recognizing and embracing these differences is essential for fostering truly inclusive and meaningful relationship practices that honor the values of all individuals involved, weaving together a broader understanding of shared human experiences. For couples seeking meaningful alternatives, here are diverse and adaptable ideas:

1. Home-Based Activities

- Cooking Together: Make a traditional or new recipe, chat while cooking, and enjoy the meal. You could also bake cookies or bread, or try making something new together. Board Games or Puzzles: Play a fun activity that promotes teamwork and laughter.
- Storytelling: Share stories about your childhood, dreams, or favorite memories.

2. Shared Hobbies or Projects

- Gardening: Work together to plant flowers, vegetables, or herbs, creating something tangible that grows over time.
- DIY Projects: Collaborate on building or crafting something together, like a craft project or home improvement task.
- Learning Together: Join an online class or workshop in a shared interest, such as cooking, arts and crafts, or painting.

3. Family-Inclusive Activities

- Outdoor Picnics: Enjoy a meal in the park or your backyard, creating a relaxing, connective environment.

- Game or Movie Nights: Include the entire family in an activity that fosters connection and fun.
- Cultural Traditions: Participate in a festival or community event together, embracing shared values and experiences that bring you closer together.

4. Outdoor Activities

- Walks Together: Take evening walks to reflect on the day and reconnect with yourself.
- Nature Exploration: Hike a trail, visit a botanical garden, or enjoy a quiet moment outdoors.
- Exercise Together: To achieve a shared health goal, consider practicing exercises like yoga, mindfulness, and strength training. Engage in light workouts or try partner exercises.

5. Intimate and Private Activities

(To nurture emotional, physical, and sensual closeness)

- Shared Shower or Bath: Enjoy a warm, relaxing shower or bath together to strengthen your connection.
- Couples Massage: Give each other massages with oils or soothing balms. This eases tension and enhances touch-based intimacy. Remember, neither of you needs to be a professional massage therapist; it's meant for fun, not perfection.
- Hydrotherapy or Spa Night: Relax in a hot tub, try steam therapy, or set up a spa-like environment at home.

- Slow Dance at Home: Play a romantic song and share a slow dance in your living room—simple yet emotionally meaningful.
- Foreplay and Intimate Exploration: Take your time to discover what brings pleasure and security to both of you.
- Enjoy Good Sex: Focus on emotional safety, communication, and being present during your physical intimacy.
- Read Song of Solomon Together: Use scripture to affirm your physical and spiritual connection.

ACTIVITY: RELATIONSHIP CHECK-UP TEMPLATE

To ensure productivity during check-ins, couples can follow this simple structure:

1. **Opening Gratitude**

- Example: "I appreciated how you supported me this week when I was feeling stressed. It made a big difference."

2. **Current Concerns**

- Example: "I've been feeling like we're not spending as much quality time together lately. I'd love to talk about how we can reconnect."

3. **Action Steps**

- Example: "What if we tried cooking dinner together

once a week? Or taking 10-minute walks after meals to talk and unwind?"

4. Future Goals

- Example: "I'd like us to plan one intentional family activity this month, like a picnic or a game night."

5. Closing Encouragement

- Example: "I'm really glad we're making time for these conversations. I feel like they're helping us grow closer."

EXERCISE: RELATIONSHIP MAINTENANCE SCHEDULE & TEMPLATE

Couples can create a personalized monthly relationship check-up template that covers the following:

- Emotional health (communication, connection, stress management)
- Physical health (intimacy, fitness, well-being)
- Financial health (budgeting, financial goals, stressors)
- Spiritual health (prayer, devotion, shared faith activities)

RELATIONSHIP CHECK-UP CONVERSATION STARTERS

General Check-in Starters:

- *"I feel like we have been really connected lately, but I'd love to hear how you're feeling about us right now."*
- *"I've noticed we've been busy with work and life. Let's talk about how we can make time for each other."*

For Soldiers Returning from Separation

- *"Coming home after being apart is always an adjustment. How are you feeling as we settle back into our routine?"*
- *"I want to hear all about your time away, but I also want to share how things have been at home. Let's take time to reconnect."*

For Long-Distance Marriages

- *"Distance makes things hard sometimes, but I appreciate our staying connected. Is there anything we can do better?"*
- *"What is one thing you have missed most about being together in person?"*

CONVERSATION EXAMPLE: A CHECK-IN ON QUALITY TIME

Setting: A couple attends their weekly relationship check-in during "Pancake Saturday."

-Opening Gratitude

- **Husband:** I appreciated your staying up to help me prepare for that presentation. Your input made all the difference.

- **Wife:** Thank you for playing soccer with the kids yesterday. Seeing them so happy makes my day better, too.

-Current Concerns

- **Wife:** I feel like we've been so busy that we haven't had much time to talk. I miss those moments where it's just us.
- **Husband:** I agree. It feels like we've been in 'go-mode' all week. I'd love to slow down and reconnect.

-Action Steps

- **Wife:** How about we cook dinner together on Wednesday? It's mid-week, giving us a break from the routine.
- **Husband:** That sounds great. I also think we could take a walk after dinner twice a week—just 15 minutes to chat.

-Future Goals

- **Husband:** Let's start with Wednesday dinners and two evening walks. If it works well, we can expand from there.
- **Wife:** Once a month, we can plan something special for the whole family, such as a movie night or a picnic.

-Closing Encouragement

- **Husband:** I love that we are both committed to giving ourselves quality time. I feel more connected already.
- **Wife:** Me too. I appreciate how open you are to these conversations. It means so much to me.

SCENARIO: RECONNECTING AFTER A STRESSFUL PERIOD

John and Lisa have been feeling distant due to their demanding work schedules. Lisa noticed that they had not had a meaningful conversation in weeks. She suggests having a relationship check-in during their usual Saturday morning breakfast.

COMPLETE CONVERSATION EXAMPLE

A Relationship Check-in Over Breakfast

-Opening Gratitude

- **Lisa:** I appreciate how you've been handling things at home while I've been busy with work. It has not gone unnoticed."
- **John:** Thanks, Lisa. I know you have a lot on your plate, and I appreciate you still making time for the kids despite your busy schedule.

-Current Concerns

- **Lisa:** I feel like we've been so busy that we haven't had a chance to talk. I miss our time together.
- **John:** Yeah, I have noticed that too. It is as if we're going through the motions instead of truly connecting.

-Action Steps

- **Lisa:** How about we set aside 30 minutes in the evening to catch up without distractions?
- **John:** That sounds good. Perhaps we could also plan a weekend activity just the two of us?

-Future Goals

- **Lisa:** Let us commit to checking in every Saturday morning. It helps keep us on track.
- **John:** "Agreed. Let's also make time for something fun together at least once a month.

-Closing Encouragement

- **Lisa:** I love that we are doing this; it makes me feel closer to you.
- **John:** Me too. I'm glad we're making our relationship a priority.

ACTIVITY: INDIVIDUAL AND COUPLE REFLECTION EXERCISE

Step 1: Personal Reflection (Individual)

- Write down one area of your relationship where you feel things are going well.
- Write down one area where you would like to see improvement.
- Reflect on how you have been contributing to the relationship's health.

- Identify one step you can take personally to enhance your connection.

Step 2: Discussion with Your Spouse

- Share one strength and one area for improvement in your relationship.
- Listen without interrupting when your spouse shares their thoughts.
- Discuss one actionable step you can commit to over the next week.

Step 3: Implementation and Check-in

- Set a date for your next relationship check-up.
- Review progress on agreed-upon action steps.
- Adjust and refine strategies as needed.

CHAPTER 5

COMMUNICATION: A PREVENTIVE TOOL
THE FOUNDATION OF A THRIVING MARRIAGE

Communication is the lifeblood of any relationship. In marriage, communication serves as the bridge that connects two individuals, enabling them to share their thoughts, feelings, needs, and dreams. However, effective communication is about speaking, listening, understanding, and connecting on a deeper level. Many couples struggle with communication, not because they lack love, but because they lack the skills to express it effectively.

Dr. Gary Chapman highlights in The 5 Love Languages (1995) that misunderstandings often arise when couples fail to communicate in ways their partner understands or values. I have also addressed these issues in my book, The 7 Apology Languages. This chapter examines the principles of effective communication, common barriers, and practical tools to enhance couples' communication skills.

PRINCIPLES OF EFFECTIVE COMMUNICATION

1. Active Listening: Active listening, a crucial skill in marriage, is more than just hearing your partner's words. It's about being fully present, engaged, and empathetic. As Dr. Harville Hendrix points out in Getting the Love You Want (1988), active listening fosters understanding. It reduces defensiveness, paving the way for a deeper, more genuine connection. By mastering this skill, couples can feel more connected and understood.

How to Practice

- Make eye contact and give your partner your full attention.
- Reflect on what they say by paraphrasing their words (e.g., "So, you're feeling frustrated because...").
- Validate their emotions, even if you do not fully agree.

2. Clarity and Directness: Being transparent and direct about your feelings and needs is key to reducing misunderstandings. Avoiding vague statements or expecting your partner to read your mind can empower you to express yourself more confidently and effectively.

- **Example:** Instead of saying, "You never help around the house," try, "I feel overwhelmed with chores and would appreciate it if we could share them more equally."

3. Gentleness and Respect: Approaching difficult conversations with gentleness and respect, as advised by Proverbs 15:1, can make you feel more at ease and less defensive. This approach fosters a more open and honest dialogue, creating a safe space for both partners to express their thoughts and feelings.

How to Practice

- Use "I" statements to express your feelings without blaming (e.g., "I feel hurt when...").
- Avoid raising your voice or using critical language.

4. Consistency in Connection: Regular, intentional communication fosters intimacy and trust. Set aside time daily or weekly to connect without distractions, allowing for meaningful conversations.

• **Example:** Spend 15 minutes each evening talking about your day or sharing something you are grateful for in your relationship.

COMMON BARRIERS TO COMMUNICATION

1. Defensiveness: When one or both partners become defensive, it shuts down open dialogue. Instead of listening, the focus shifts to self-protection, leading to misunderstandings, unresolved issues, and emotional distance that ultimately strain the relationship.

• **How to Overcome:** Pause and reflect on your partner's perspective before responding. Practice self-awareness and humility.

2. Stonewalling: Stonewalling, or emotionally withdrawing during a conversation, creates distance and frustration. Dr. John Gottman identifies stonewalling as one of the "Four Horsemen of the Apocalypse" that predict divorce (*The Seven Principles for Making Marriage Work*, 1999).

• **How to Overcome:** Take a break if emotions run high, but commit to revisiting the conversation when both partners are calm and composed.

3. Assumptions and Misinterpretations: Assuming your partner's intentions or jumping to conclusions often leads to misunderstandings.

• **How to Overcome:** Seek clarification by asking questions (e.g., "Can you explain what you meant by that?").

4. Distractions: External distractions, such as phones, work, or children, can interrupt meaningful communication.

• **How to Overcome:** Create distraction-free zones or times, such as during meals or scheduled check-ins.

5. Resentment and Unforgiveness: Resentment and unforgiveness create emotional barriers that hinder open and honest communication. Holding onto past grievances fosters bitterness, making it difficult to engage in healthy dialogue. When left unresolved, these emotions can lead to emotional detachment and escalate minor conflicts into more severe marital issues.

• **How to Overcome**

- Address unresolved issues early rather than letting them fester.
- Practice forgiveness as an intentional choice, even when emotions say otherwise.
- Engage in open and honest conversations to clarify misunderstandings and establish clear expectations.

- Pray together for healing and reconciliation, allowing spiritual guidance to lead the process.

HOW TO LISTEN TO UNDERSTAND, NOT JUST RESPOND

Listening to understand, rather than simply responding, is one of the most crucial skills in effective communication. Too often, conversations become battlegrounds where partners focus on crafting their next reply instead of truly hearing what the other person is saying. This can lead to misunderstandings, frustration, and emotional distance.

1. The Difference Between Hearing and Understanding:
Hearing is a passive process; understanding is an active one. When you truly listen, you absorb the words, emotions, and intent behind them. You focus on grasping your partner's feelings rather than formulating your rebuttal.

- **Example:** If your spouse says, "I feel like we don't spend much time together anymore," listening to understand means recognizing the emotion behind the words (loneliness or longing) rather than immediately getting defensive.

2. Techniques for Listening to Understand

- **Practice Active Listening:** Maintain eye contact, nod occasionally, and use affirmations like "I see" or "That makes sense."
- **Pause Before Responding:** Take a moment to process what your partner has said before formulating a response.
- **Reflect:** Repeat or rephrase what you heard to ensure you understood correctly. (e.g., "So, you're

feeling unappreciated because of how busy things have been?")

- **Ask Clarifying Questions:** Instead of assuming, ask, "Can you tell me more about what you mean?"

3. The Power of Emotional Validation: Validation means acknowledging your partner's feelings, even if you do not necessarily agree with them.

- **Example:** "I understand you are feeling overwhelmed with work right now. That must be stressful. How can I support you?" By adopting this mindset, couples create a safe emotional space for genuine connection and problem-solving, where both partners feel secure and understood.

THE POWER OF WORDS: ENCOURAGING VS. DESTRUCTIVE SPEECH

Words hold immense power in shaping the emotional climate of a marriage. Proverbs 18:21 states, "The tongue has the power of life and death," highlighting the ability of speech to either build up or tear down relationships.

1. Encouraging Words: Building Each Other Up: Encouraging words are a powerful way to reinforce love, appreciation, and respect in marriage. By using simple affirmations, you can significantly enhance your partner's sense of value, fostering a more profound understanding of gratitude and respect in your relationship.

Examples

- "I appreciate everything you do for our family."

- "You inspire me with how dedicated you are to your work and our home."
- "I love how you make me laugh even on tough days."

Regularly affirming your spouse fosters emotional security and strengthens marital bonds.

2. Destructive Speech: Words That Tear Down: Negative words, especially during conflict, can cause deep wounds that linger long after an argument ends.

Examples of Destructive Speech:

- **Criticism:** "You never help around the house!"
- **Contempt:** "I don't know why I even bother talking to you."
- **Blaming:** "This is all your fault."
- **Sarcasm:** "Oh, sure, because you're *so* perfect."

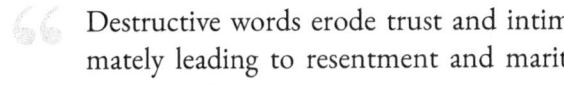 Destructive words erode trust and intimacy, ultimately leading to resentment and marital bitterness over time.

3. Replacing Destructive Speech with Encouraging Speech: If a conversation starts to head toward negativity, pause and intentionally shift your tone to a more constructive one.

Example: Instead of saying, "You never listen to me!" try, "I need to feel heard right now. Can we take a moment to talk?" By intentionally using words to uplift rather than tear down, couples create an atmosphere of love, trust, and emotional safety in their marriage.

PRACTICAL TOOLS FOR EFFECTIVE COMMUNICATION

1. The Speaker-Listener Technique: This structured approach allows each partner to speak and be heard without interruption.

How It Works

- One partner speaks while the other listens without interrupting.
- The listener reflects on what they heard to ensure understanding.
- Switch roles and repeat until both feel understood.

2. Check-in Questions: Use intentional questions to foster connection and understanding.

Examples

- "What's been on your mind lately?"
- "How can I support you better this week?"
- "What's one thing I did recently that made you feel loved?"

3. Shared Communication Rituals: Create regular rituals that encourage open dialogue.

Examples

- Weekly coffee dates at home to discuss goals or challenges.

- Evening walks are an opportunity to reflect on the day.
- Gratitude journaling together, sharing one entry each night.

4. The Time-Out Strategy: When emotions escalate, take a time-out to cool off before continuing the conversation.

How to Practice

- Establish a "time-out" code word with your partner.
- Agree to revisit the topic after a set amount of time (e.g., 20 minutes).

EFFECTIVE COMMUNICATION STRATEGIES FOR LONG-DISTANCE MARITAL RELATIONSHIPS

Whether due to work, military deployment, or training, long-distance marriages require intentional communication to maintain intimacy and trust. Physical separation can create emotional distance if communication is inconsistent or ineffective. However, couples who develop structured communication strategies can strengthen their relationship despite the miles between them.

1. Establish Consistent Check-ins

- Set specific times for daily or weekly calls to maintain an emotional connection.
- Utilize multiple communication channels, such as video calls, voice notes, and written letters, to maintain varied and meaningful interactions.

- Respect each other's schedules by coordinating the best times for both partners to ensure a mutually beneficial arrangement.

2. Prioritize Quality Over Quantity

- Rather than focusing on the number of conversations, ensure each interaction is meaningful.
- Ask open-ended questions like, "What has been the highlight of your day?" or "What's something new you've been thinking about?"
- Share personal updates, thoughts, and reflections rather than logistical details.

3. Use Technology to Stay Emotionally Engaged

- Share daily moments through photos, videos, or voice recordings.
- To create shared experiences, consider playing online games together, watching the same movie, or listening to the same podcast.
- Utilize relationship apps that allow partners to send virtual notes, schedule future dates, and keep relationship reminders.

4. Manage Expectations and Plan for Reunions

- Be upfront about challenges and concerns, ensuring both partners feel heard and understood.
- Discuss emotional and physical expectations while apart, including ways to maintain intimacy and connection.

- Plan visits or future reunions so you have something to look forward to and reaffirm your commitment to each other.

5. Address Conflicts Proactively

- Misunderstandings are common in long-distance relationships due to the lack of nonverbal cues. Always clarify rather than assume.
- When tensions arise, take a moment to process your emotions before discussing your concerns.
- Use "I" statements to express feelings without placing blame (e.g., "I feel disconnected when we don't talk for days" instead of "You never make time for me").

6. Keep the Romance Alive

- Send handwritten letters or surprise gifts to express love and appreciation.
- Celebrate milestones and special occasions creatively, even from a distance.
- Plan virtual date nights with intentional activities such as cooking the same meal or stargazing over video chat.

By implementing these strategies, couples in long-distance marriages can cultivate emotional closeness, strengthen trust, and maintain a healthy relationship despite physical separation.

SAMPLE CONVERSATION: NAVIGATING A MISUNDERSTANDING

A couple has been arguing about household responsibilities. During their scheduled communication time, they decide to address the issue.

- **Husband:** I have been taking on more household tasks lately, which has been overwhelming. I know you've been busy, but I could use some help.
- **Wife:** I didn't realize you felt that way. I've been so focused on work that I didn't notice you were feeling overwhelmed. Thank you for bringing it up.
- **Husband:** I know your job has been demanding lately, and I appreciate everything you're doing. We could work together to strike a better balance.
- **Wife:** I agree. Let's list tasks and divide them so they feel more manageable for both of us. Maybe we can check in weekly to see how it's going. That sounds like a great idea. Thank you for being willing to work on this with me.

SAMPLE CONVERSATION FOR LONG-DISTANCE RELATIONSHIP: NAVIGATING A MISUNDERSTANDING

A husband and wife are in a long-distance marriage due to the husband's military deployment. Lately, communication has felt strained, and emotions are running high.

- **Husband:** I feel like our conversations have been getting shorter, and I miss feeling truly connected with you. I know you're busy, but I just wanted to bring it up because it's been on my mind.

- **Wife:** I appreciate you telling me that. Honestly, I've been feeling the same way. With the time zone difference and our schedules, I think we've been rushing through our calls.
- **Husband:** Exactly. I also don't want you to feel pressured to talk when you're exhausted, but I'd love to find a way to have more meaningful conversations.
- **Wife:** That makes sense. Maybe instead of trying to talk every night when I am drained, we could schedule longer conversations three times a week and check in with voice notes on the other days?
- **Husband:** I love that idea. That way, we can still stay connected without feeling overwhelmed.
- **Wife:** And maybe we could also set a time for virtual dates—like watching a movie together or cooking the same meal while on a video call?
- **Husband:** That sounds perfect. I appreciate your willingness to work on this with me.

Activity: Communication Assessment
1. Individual Reflection

- Write down one area where you feel communication could improve in your marriage.
- Reflect on how you currently handle discussions in that area.

2. Partner Discussion

- Share your reflections with your spouse and listen to their perspective without interrupting.

- Discuss how you can improve communication together.

3. Set Goals

- Agree on one or two specific goals, such as practicing active listening or scheduling weekly check-ins.

SUMMARY

Communication is essential for a strong marriage. Couples should embrace active listening. Engaging in kind and clear conversations is crucial. They should also address common obstacles. This approach helps strengthen their bond and positively resolve conflicts. Effective communication fosters trust, intimacy, and a shared vision for the future. In the next chapter, we will explore conflict resolution strategies. We will learn how to turn disagreements into opportunities for growth and deeper understanding.

CHAPTER 6

MARITAL CONFLICT RESOLUTION
NAVIGATING DISAGREEMENTS WITH LOVE AND WISDOM

C onflict is inevitable in marriage, a natural occurrence that does not signify a failing relationship. Instead, how couples navigate these disagreements shapes their marital health, stability, and longevity. Many conflicts stem from differences in personality, values, upbringing, and expectations, underscoring the importance of couples cultivating practical conflict-resolution skills. This chapter explores the nature of conflict in marriage, unhealthy conflict patterns, practical steps for resolution, and the role of faith in handling marital disagreements.

Research indicates that resolving disagreements constructively and respectfully is a strong predictor of long-term marital satisfaction (*Fincham & Beach, 2020*). Couples who avoid confrontation or engage in unhealthy communication patterns often face growing resentment, emotional disconnection, and increased stress. However, when conflict is managed with wisdom, love, and biblical principles, it becomes an opportunity for deeper understanding, trust, and intimacy.

The Bible serves as a beacon of guidance on handling conflict in a manner that fosters reconciliation rather than division. Ephesians 4:26 advises, "In your anger do not sin: Do not let the sun go down while you are still angry," stressing the importance of promptly addressing disputes with a heart of reconciliation. Similarly, Colossians 3:13 encourages believers to "bear with each other and forgive one another if any of you has a grievance against someone. Forgive as the Lord forgave you." These biblical principles provide a solid foundation for managing marital disagreements.

THE NATURE OF CONFLICT IN MARRIAGE

Understanding the nature and causes of conflict in a relationship is a powerful tool for growth and improvement. It empowers couples to address disagreements proactively, preventing them from escalating into major marital issues. Conflict can stem from various sources, some minor and easily resolved, others deeply rooted in emotions, values, and long-standing beliefs. While every relationship is unique, research shows that the most common causes of conflict in marriage include the following:

1. Communication Differences: Miscommunication is one of the most frequent sources of marital tension. It involves misunderstandings, a lack of listening, or assumptions about each other's intent. Each partner brings a unique communication style into the marriage, often shaped by their family of origin and past experiences.

Misunderstandings arise when one spouse prefers direct and logical discussions while the other values emotional expression and connection. The lack of active listening, tone misinterpretations, and assumptions about intent can escalate minor disagreements into significant conflicts. It can arise from:

- **Different communication styles** – One spouse prefers direct and logical discussions, while the other values emotional expression.
- **Failure to actively listen** – Responding instead of **understanding** leads to frustration.
- **Non-verbal misunderstandings** – Tone, facial expressions, and body language can be misinterpreted.

Solution

- Develop active listening skills.
- Listen to understand and not to respond.
- Seek clarity before reacting.
- Be quick to listen, slow to speak, and slow to become angry (James 1:19).

2. Financial Issues: Disagreements over spending, saving, debt, or financial priorities. Research by *Dew and Stewart (2019)* found that financial disagreements are one of the strongest predictors of divorce. Conflicts related to spending habits, saving priorities, debt management, and financial transparency can create significant tension, especially when one spouse is a saver and the other a spender. Financial responsibilities to extended family, especially in cultures where supporting relatives is expected, can lead to numerous marital disagreements. Common financial conflicts include:

- Differing attitudes toward spending vs. saving.
- Disparities in income and financial contributions.
- Extended family financial obligations (sending money overseas, family expectations, or inheritance disputes).

Solution

- Establish financial transparency.
- Create a shared budget.
- Set clear financial goals together.

3. Parenting Styles and Family Expectations: Parenting styles and family expectations frequently become points of contention. Differences in discipline methods, educational priorities, and family involvement in child-rearing can create strain, particularly if the couple did not discuss their parenting philosophies before marriage. Differences in parenting beliefs are often shaped by:

- Upbringing and childhood experiences.
- Cultural and religious perspectives on parenting.
- Influence of extended family and in-laws.

Solution

- Discuss parenting expectations before conflicts arise.
- Agree on consistent discipline and parenting approaches.
- No matter what, do not let the kids divide you.
- Work as a team with one voice and refrain from trying to counter each other.

(*Source: Whisman et al., 2023, "Family Influence on Marital Conflict"*)

4. Household Responsibilities and Gender Roles: Conflicts over chores and responsibilities often arise when one spouse feels burdened or unappreciated. Conflicts over household responsibilities and gender roles typically arise when expectations regarding work, caregiving, and domestic duties are misaligned or unbalanced. This is especially common in households where:

- One spouse expects traditional gender roles (e.g., the husband provides for the family while the wife handles household duties).
- Both partners work full-time, but only one of them contributes to household chores.
- There is inequality in emotional or mental labor, such as managing schedules, childcare, or family obligations.

Solution

- Divide responsibilities fairly.
- Respect both work and household contributions.
- Be flexible, selfless, and valuable.
- If you see a need, address it.

Research suggests that equitable division of labor leads to higher marital satisfaction (*Carlson et al., 2022*).

5. Emotional Disconnection and Unmet Expectations: Unspoken expectations in marriage often lead to disappointment, resentment, and emotional distance. Unmet expectations may include:

- **Affection and quality time** – One spouse expects regular emotional check-ins, while the other prioritizes independence.

- **Career and personal growth support**: A spouse may feel unsupported in their ambitions.
- **Relational expectations** – Assumptions about how often to communicate, resolve conflicts, or express love.
- **Feelings of Neglect**: Feelings of being unheard, unappreciated, or emotionally neglected.

Unmet expectations in marriage are another major contributor to conflict. Many individuals enter marriage with assumptions about love, support, and shared responsibilities, only to find that their partner has a different outlook. Expectations regarding affection, quality time, career ambitions, and emotional support must be clearly communicated and adjusted as needed. Failure to do so can lead to frustration and disappointment.

Solution

- Clear and regular communication of expectations is crucial. It ensures mutual understanding and alignment, preventing unmet expectations from becoming a major contributor to conflict in marriage (*Fincham & Beach, 2021*).
- Do you feel any way about your marriage? Communicate it.
- Please do not use your unmet expectations to counter your spouse's unmet expectations; it will only lead to a negative outcome.
- Prioritize mutual understanding over one-sided understanding.

6. Cultural Differences and Conflicting Worldviews: These two factors also affect marital conflict, particularly in intercultural marriages. Differences in relationship roles, religious beliefs, and approaches to conflict resolution can create misunderstandings if not addressed with openness and mutual respect (*Xu & Burleson, 2020*). For intercultural couples or partners raised in different environments, differences in worldview can create tension. Conflicts may stem from:

- Differing views on marriage roles (e.g., traditional vs. modern perspectives).
- Religious and spiritual differences affect daily life.
- Different approaches to conflict resolution include direct confrontation versus indirect discussion.

In some cultures, public displays of affection are expected, while in others, they may be considered disrespectful. Such differences can lead to misinterpretations of intentions and emotional needs.

Solution

- Learn about each other's cultural backgrounds.
- Create a shared understanding of what works best for the relationship (Xu & Burleson, 2020).
- Do not try to change your spouse; appreciate their uniqueness.
- Understand how their culture and worldview shape their understanding of various topics and issues.
- Respecting each other's cultural backgrounds, values, and worldviews.

7. Differences in Intimacy Needs: Physical intimacy is a significant aspect of marriage, and conflict can arise when couples fail to align their expectations of intimacy. Disagreements may stem from:

- Differences in libido or intimacy preferences.
- Cultural or religious beliefs about sex in marriage.
- Unresolved emotional conflicts affect physical intimacy.

When intimacy needs are not addressed, it can lead to feelings of rejection, insecurity, or emotional distance.

Solution

- Maintain open and respectful conversations about intimacy needs.
- Try as much as possible to learn what sexual satisfaction means to your spouse.
- Understand your own and your spouse's body language to avoid conflict in the communication of intimacy or sex.
- Ensure that both of you feel valued and understood (*Johnson & Zuccarini, 2021*).

8. Conflicts Involving Extended Family and In-Laws:
When family members exert influence over a marriage, conflicts can arise. Typical in-law and family-related conflicts include:

- Over-involvement in decision-making.
- Comparisons with other family members.
- Pressure to conform to family traditions.

Solution

- Prioritize the marriage by establishing clear boundaries with external family members. (*Genesis 2:24* – "A man shall leave his father and mother and be united to his wife").

- Maintain a united front and have united decisions.
- Avoid arguing about in-laws in front of them.
- Do not prioritize your extended family over your spouse, like siblings, parents, or in-laws.

(*Source: Whisman et al., 2023, "Family Influence on Marital Conflict"*)

WHY SOME CONFLICTS ESCALATE

Some conflicts become deeply destructive due to poor communication, unresolved past hurts, or unhealthy patterns of conflict resolution. Unresolved conflict can lead to:

- **Emotional withdrawal** – One or both partners shutting down.
- **Resentment and bitterness** – Holding grudges instead of seeking healing.
- **Escalation into hostility** – Anger turning into verbal or emotional abuse.

Understanding the root causes of conflict enables couples to address disagreements with wisdom and clarity, rather than letting them spiral into division.

Breaking the Cycle of Unhealthy Conflict

- Replace criticism with gentle expressions of feelings and needs.
- Replace defensiveness with active listening and accountability.
- Replace contempt with respect and appreciation.

- Replace stonewalling with engagement and problem-solving.

(*Source: Gottman & Silver, 2022, "The Seven Principles for Making Marriage Work"*)

STEPS TO RESOLVING CONFLICT CONSTRUCTIVELY

Step 1: Create a Safe Space for Honest Communication

- Avoid discussing issues when emotions are high; instead, choose a calm moment to address them.
- Set ground rules (no yelling, no insults, no walking away).
- Use *"I" statements* instead of *"You" accusations* (e.g., *"I feel unheard when my concerns are dismissed"* instead of *"You never listen to me!"*).

Step 2: Listen to Understand, Not Just to Respond

- Active listening: Make eye contact, nod, and paraphrase what your spouse is saying before responding.
- Ask clarifying questions to prevent misunderstandings.
- Resist the urge to interrupt or jump to conclusions.

Step 3: Identify the Real Issue Behind the Conflict

- Sometimes, surface-level arguments mask deeper concerns.

Ask: *"Is this argument really about money, or do I feel like my needs are not being prioritized?"*

Step 4: Find a Solution Together

The goal is not to "win" the argument but to win together as a couple.

- List out possible solutions and find common ground.
- Compromise where possible while ensuring both partners feel respected and valued.

Step 5: Apologize and Forgive

- Apologies should be genuine and specific (*"I'm sorry for raising my voice; I should have spoken more calmly"*).
- Forgiveness does not mean forgetting but letting go of resentment and moving forward (*Colossians 3:13*).

(*Source: Fincham & Beach, 2021, "Conflict Resolution in Marriage: A Psychological Perspective"*)

THE 7 APOLOGY LANGUAGES

One of the most overlooked aspects of conflict resolution is the art of apology. Many couples struggle to move past conflicts because they do not fully grasp how their spouse receives and interprets apologies. While Dr. Gary Chapman popularized the Five Apology Languages, my research expands on this with seven distinct apology languages that more comprehensively address marital reconciliation.

i. **Expressing Regret** – Saying "I'm sorry" with sincerity and acknowledging the emotional pain that has been caused.
ii. **Accepting Responsibility** – Admitting fault without excuses or blame-shifting.
iii. **Genuine Repentance** – Showing a desire to change and not repeat the mistake.
iv. **Making Amends** – Offering tangible actions to restore trust.
v. **Requesting Forgiveness** – Explicitly asking, "Will you forgive me?"
vi. **Recognizing the Depth of Hurt** – Acknowledging the gravity of the pain inflicted.
vii. **Demonstrating Change Over Time** – Proving through consistent actions that lessons have been learned. Each spouse may resonate with different apology languages, and understanding this can significantly enhance conflict resolution and reconciliation.

HANDLING CONFLICT INVOLVING EXTENDED FAMILY (E.G., IN-LAWS)

Many marital conflicts stem from external family influence, especially when in-laws or extended relatives become too involved in personal matters.

Common In-Law Conflicts

- Over-involvement in decisions (e.g., parenting choices, finances).

- Comparisons to other couples or family members.
- Cultural or generational differences in expectations of marriage roles.

Solution: Setting Boundaries with Love

- Prioritize your marriage: *"A man shall leave his father and mother and be united to his wife"* (*Genesis 2:24*).
- Communicate Boundaries. You should agree on what is acceptable and unacceptable regarding family involvement.
- Present a United Front. Avoid arguing about in-laws before them. Address issues privately as a couple.

(*Source: Whisman et al., 2023, "Family Influence on Marital Conflict"*)

EXAMPLE CONFLICT RESOLUTION CONVERSATION: HANDLING A MISCARRIAGE

Lisa and John recently experienced a miscarriage. John copes by staying busy, while Lisa wants to talk and process their grief together. She feels abandoned, while John feels overwhelmed.

Lisa: *I feel like I'm carrying this loss alone. Please talk to me about it.*
John: *I don't know what to say. I don't want to make it worse.*
Lisa: *I do not need you to fix it. I need to know you are with me in this pain.*
John: *I hear you. I will try to discuss it further. Can we start by praying together?*

Why It Works

- Lisa expresses her feelings without attacking John.
- John acknowledges her pain without getting defensive.
- They find a solution together through prayer and open discussion.

(*Source: Harris et al., 2024, "Marriage and Trauma Recovery"*)

HANDLING CONFLICT IN LONG-DISTANCE MARRIAGES

Long-distance marriages present unique challenges that require intentional communication, trust, and emotional resilience. Whether due to military deployment, work relocation, or educational pursuits, the absence of daily physical presence can exacerbate conflicts if not adequately managed. The lack of face-to-face interaction can lead to misinterpretations, emotional disconnection, and even a sense of loneliness or insecurity. These are common conflicts in long-distance marriages.

1. **Miscommunication and Assumptions –**
   Without physical presence, nuances in tone, facial expressions, and gestures are lost, increasing the likelihood of misunderstandings. Text-based communication, in particular, can be easily misinterpreted, leading to unnecessary conflicts and misunderstandings.
2. **Emotional Distance and Loneliness**—Physical absence can result in feelings of neglect, causing one or both partners to feel disconnected and

unimportant. If not addressed proactively, this can lead to resentment.

3. **Jealousy and Trust Issues** – Extended periods of separation can foster feelings of insecurity, making one or both spouses vulnerable to doubt, suspicion, or jealousy. Without trust, even minor concerns can escalate into significant conflicts.

4. **Unmet Expectations for Communication** – One spouse may expect frequent check-ins, while the other prefers occasional updates. Differences in communication frequency or depth can create frustration and misunderstandings.

5. **Financial Disputes** – Managing finances separately or differences in financial priorities may lead to disagreements, especially if travel expenses and shared costs are not discussed in advance.

STRATEGIES FOR RESOLVING CONFLICT IN LONG-DISTANCE MARRIAGES

Conflict resolution presents unique challenges for military couples or those in geographically separated marriages. Here are strategies to maintain connection and resolve conflicts effectively:

1. Schedule Regular Check-ins – Plan structured times for deep conversations about emotions, concerns, and expectations. These intentional moments of connection help maintain emotional closeness despite physical distance.

Schedule Conflict-Resolution Calls Thoughtfully

- Avoid discussing sensitive topics when stressed or distracted.
- Set a time when both partners can focus and respond calmly to each other.

2. Use Video Calls Whenever Possible—Seeing each other's facial expressions and hearing the tone of voice adds depth to conversations and minimizes misunderstandings. Make time for quality virtual interactions.

3. Clarify Communication Expectations – Discuss and agree on how often you will communicate to avoid unmet expectations. Understanding each other's communication needs prevents feelings of neglect or smothering.

4. Use Technology to Enhance Connection—Utilize video calls for difficult conversations instead of relying solely on text. Leave voice notes if discussing sensitive issues to preserve tone and intent.

Practice Digital Conflict Resolution – Avoid arguing through text messages. When tension arises, opt for a phone or video call to prevent misinterpretations and resolve conflicts more effectively.

5. Build Trust Through Transparency – Share your daily activities, challenges, and plans openly to maintain a strong connection. Honesty about struggles and experiences fosters deeper emotional intimacy.

6. Reassure One Another Frequently – Words of affirmation become even more critical in long-distance relationships. Reassuring your spouse that they are loved, valued, and appreciated helps combat feelings of insecurity.

7. Clarify Intentions and Avoid Assumptions - Misinterpreting text messages is common; clarify before reacting. For example: "Did you mean it this way, or did I misread?"

8. Reaffirm Commitment Despite Distance - Frequent reassurances of love and commitment prevent feelings of detachment. Plan virtual date nights or fun times to maintain emotional intimacy and connection.

9. Prioritize Reunions and Quality Time Together – When possible, create special memories when reuniting. Quality time together, free from distractions, strengthens the bond and reinforces emotional and physical intimacy.

BIBLICAL WISDOM FOR LONG-DISTANCE MARITAL CONFLICT

• *1 Corinthians 13:4-7* – "Love is patient, love is kind... it always protects, always trusts, always hopes, always perseveres." This scripture reminds couples that love requires patience, trust, and resilience —essential qualities in long-distance marriages.

• *Ecclesiastes 4:9-10* – "Two are better than one... If either of them falls, one can help the other up." Even when physically apart, spouses must support each other, offering encouragement and emotional security.

• *Proverbs 3:5-6* – "Trust in the Lord with all your heart and lean not on your understanding." Maintaining faith and trusting in God's plan can provide comfort and strength during times of separation. When couples implement these strategies and keep faith at the center of their relationship, they can navigate conflicts effectively while maintaining strong emotional and spiritual connections in long-distance marriages.

BIBLICAL PERSPECTIVE ON HANDLING CONFLICT

The Bible provides wisdom on approaching and resolving disagreements in a way that strengthens, rather than weakens, the marital bond. Here are key biblical principles for handling conflict constructively:

1 Speak with Grace and Wisdom

The tone of your words is just as important as the words themselves.

- Proverbs 15:1: "A gentle answer turns away wrath, but a harsh word stirs up anger."
- Harsh words escalate conflict, while gentle responses defuse tension.

2. Resolve Conflict Quickly

- Ephesians 4:26-27: "Do not let the sun go down while you are still angry, and do not give the devil a foothold."
- Lingering anger can create bitterness and emotional distance. While not all disagreements can be resolved immediately, couples should commit to addressing and resolving their conflicts rather than ignoring or burying them.

3 Seek Understanding Over Being Right

- James 1:19-20: "Everyone should be quick to listen, slow to speak, and slow to become angry because human anger does not produce the righteousness that God desires."

- A marriage thrives when both partners prioritize listening over defending their positions.

4 Forgive as Christ Forgave

- Colossians 3:13: "Bear with each other and forgive one another if you have a grievance against someone. Forgive as the Lord forgave you."
- True forgiveness is an act of grace that releases resentment and allows healing to take root in your heart.

5 Seek Wise Counsel When Needed

- Proverbs 11:14: "Where there is no guidance, a people falls, but in an abundance of counselors there is safety."
- Seeking guidance from trusted mentors, pastors, or counselors can provide clarity and perspective when navigating complex conflicts.

James 1:19-20 states: "Everyone should be quick to listen, slow to speak, and slow to become angry, because human anger does not produce the righteousness that God desires." This verse serves as a foundational guideline for managing conflict effectively.

1. Quick to Listen: Practicing Active Listening

- Avoid interrupting; let your partner fully express their thoughts and ideas.

- Use paraphrasing to ensure understanding: "So, you're saying that..."
- Validate emotions: "I hear that this made you feel..."

2. Slow to Speak: Thoughtful and Constructive Responses

- Pause before responding to avoid reacting emotionally.
- Use "I" statements instead of blame: "I feel hurt when..." instead of "You always..."
- Keep the tone gentle and respectful (Proverbs 15:1: "A gentle answer turns away wrath...").

3. Slow to Anger: Emotional Regulation and Patience

- Recognize personal triggers and practice self-control.
- Take a step back if emotions are escalating rather than lashing out.
- Pray together or individually for wisdom before continuing a heated discussion.

COOLING-OFF AGREEMENT TEMPLATE

For moments when emotions run high, couples can use a *Cooling-Off Agreement* to prevent conflicts from escalating into hurtful exchanges. This template provides a structured way to pause and revisit the conversation when both partners are ready.

Cooling-Off Agreement Purpose: To give both partners time to process emotions before engaging in conflict resolution.

1 . Recognize the Need for a Break: Either partner can request a pause if emotions are escalating.

- *Phrase to use:* "I need a moment to cool off so I can respond with love and understanding."

2. Agree on a Set Time to Revisit the Discussion

- Agree on a time (e.g., "Let us talk in 30 minutes" or "Let us discuss this tomorrow morning").

3. Use the Time to Reflect, Not Ruminate: Reflect on emotions, assumptions, and possible solutions.

- Engage in calming activities such as prayer, journaling, or walking.

4. Return with a Willingness to Listen

- Approach the discussion with a commitment to finding a solution, not proving a point.
- Use "I" statements and reaffirm your commitment to a peaceful resolution.

ACTIVITY: CONFLICT RESOLUTION REFLECTION & APPLICATION

1. Self-Assessment

- What are my top three conflict triggers?
- How do I usually respond when conflict arises?
- What areas do I need to improve?

2. Partner Discussion

- Share your reflections and discuss patterns in your conflicts.
- Identify one change each partner will commit to for better conflict resolution.

3. Journaling Prompts

- How did I handle my last disagreement with my spouse?
- What could I have done differently?
- How can I apply biblical principles to my approach to conflict resolution?

CONCLUSION

Conflict in marriage is inevitable, but when handled wisely, it can lead to greater understanding, emotional connection, and relational growth. By practicing effective communication, emotional intelligence, and biblical wisdom, couples can turn disagreements into opportunities for deeper intimacy.

CHAPTER 7

RELATIONAL GRATITUDE
STRENGTHENING YOUR MARRIAGE THROUGH APPRECIATION

Gratitude is a vital yet often overlooked aspect of a strong and thriving marriage. Amid life's busyness, couples may unintentionally neglect each other, focusing more on unmet expectations than appreciating the positives already in their relationship. Gratitude is one of the most underrated yet powerful tools in marriage. A grateful heart cultivates a positive environment, strengthens bonds, and deepens intimacy between spouses. This chapter aims to rekindle a culture of gratitude in marriage—one that fosters appreciation, acknowledgment, and recognition of each partner's contributions. Studies in positive psychology suggest that practicing gratitude in relationships can improve emotional connection, reduce stress, and increase overall marital satisfaction (Algoe et al., 2010).

While many couples start their marriage full of appreciation, over time, daily routines, responsibilities, and challenges can cause them to take each other for granted. When couples actively nurture appreciation for one another, they reinforce the foundation of their marriage, making it more resilient against external pressures and internal conflicts. Research also shows that practicing gratitude can enhance marital satisfaction, foster deeper emotional bonds, and reduce resentment (Emmons & McCullough, 2003).

THE ROLE OF GRATITUDE IN A THRIVING MARRIAGE

Gratitude is more than saying "thank you." It is an intentional mindset that recognizes and appreciates your spouse's efforts, qualities, and presence in your life. When couples practice gratitude, they shift their focus from what is missing to what is already present, creating a culture of appreciation rather than expectation. This can be as simple as a daily 'thank you' for a specific action or a heartfelt acknowledgment of your partner's qualities during a difficult time.

BENEFITS OF PRACTICING GRATITUDE IN MARRIAGE

1. Strengthens Emotional Connection
Expressing appreciation fosters warmth, trust, and intimacy between spouses. When one feels valued, they are more likely to open their heart, creating an emotionally secure marriage.

2. Encourages Positive Reinforcement
Gratitude motivates a spouse to continue their loving actions. When people feel appreciated for their actions, they are naturally inclined to do more of it. A simple "thank you" can make all the difference in reinforcing positive behaviors.

3. Reduces Conflict and Resentment
When gratitude becomes a habit, couples are less likely to dwell on disappointments. Instead of nitpicking flaws, they focus on their spouse's positive contributions, which reduces unnecessary conflicts.

4. Increases Marital Satisfaction

Studies show that couples who regularly express appreciation for one another report higher levels of happiness and contentment in their marriage (Algoe, Fredrickson, & Gable, 2013).

5. Strengthens the Marital Bond

Gratitude fosters a "us against the world" mentality rather than a "me versus you" mentality. It reminds couples that they are a team, strengthening their commitment and resilience as they face life's challenges together. Gratitude reminds couples of the good in their spouse, reinforcing positive feelings and admiration. Couples who regularly express appreciation report higher levels of marital satisfaction (Gordon et al., 2012).

6. Fosters the Spirit of Oneness

When spouses express gratitude toward each other, they reinforce the idea that they are not separate individuals working in opposition but one united entity. This deepens mutual understanding, fosters trust, and strengthens their shared purpose in marriage. Encourages Mutual Respect and Oneness. Viewing each other as teammates rather than competitors fosters unity and camaraderie. Gratitude shifts the focus from what is lacking to what is being contributed in the relationship.

7. Attracts the Presence and Favor of God

A grateful heart invites contentment, joy, and divine blessings into the relationship. Gratitude aligns with biblical principles and invites God's blessings into the marriage. The Bible states in 1 Thessalonians 5:18, "Give thanks in all circumstances; for this is the will of God in Christ Jesus for you." A grateful heart pleases God, and when gratitude is practiced in marriage, it creates an atmosphere where God's love and favor can flourish.

8. Improves Mental and Emotional Well-Being

Gratitude is associated with reduced stress and enhanced emotional well-being (Emmons & McCullough, 2003). A grateful spouse is generally happier and more content, making them better equipped to handle challenges with patience and grace. Expressing appreciation lowers stress, anxiety, and depression in both partners. Gratitude promotes emotional regulation and enhances overall well-being.

9. Encourages Selflessness and Generosity

When a spouse feels genuinely appreciated, they are more likely to reciprocate by being generous with their time, love, and service. Gratitude shifts the mindset from "What am I getting?" to "What can I give?" fostering mutual care and support.

10. Creates a Cycle of Joy and Appreciation

When expressed, appreciation encourages more acts of kindness and affection. Appreciation reinforces a cycle of positivity. A marriage grounded in gratitude fosters a positive cycle—one spouse's appreciation sparks more loving actions, which in turn inspire further gratitude. This cycle cultivates a joyful and fulfilling relationship.

THE DANGERS OF INGRATITUDE IN MARRIAGE

A lack of gratitude in marriage can slowly erode love, intimacy, and emotional connection. When couples fail to recognize and appreciate each other, the following negative patterns can emerge:

1. Feelings of Being Undervalued

- One or both partners may feel unseen, unheard, or taken for granted.
- Over time, this leads to emotional detachment and resentment.

2. Increased Marital Conflict

- Ingratitude fosters a negative perception of one's spouse, leading to frustration and blame.
- Minor irritations become major conflicts when appreciation is absent.

3. A Culture of Entitlement

- When gratitude is replaced with entitlement, couples expect rather than appreciate.
- The focus shifts to what is lacking rather than what is given, diminishing contentment.

4. Reduced Intimacy and Connection

- Emotional distance grows when spouses fail to express love, admiration, and appreciation for one another.
- Physical and emotional intimacy suffer as a result.

THE DANGER OF COMPARISON IN MARRIAGE

One of the greatest threats to relational gratitude is the tendency to compare one's spouse or marriage to others. Social media, Hollywood romances, and cultural expectations often create unrealistic standards that leave couples feeling dissatisfied with their reality. When one spouse constantly measures their partner against an outside standard, whether it be another couple, societal norms, or a past relationship, it plants seeds of dissatisfaction that can erode trust, intimacy, and joy in marriage.

Comparing ourselves to others can be detrimental for several reasons. It can lead to feelings of inadequacy and low self-esteem, as we often focus on what others have that we lack. This mindset can lead to unnecessary stress and anxiety, making it challenging to appreciate our unique qualities and accomplishments. Instead of fostering a healthy sense of self, comparison can create a sense of competition and resentment. Recognizing our journeys and celebrating our progress, rather than measuring our worth against someone else's standards, is essential.

1. It Creates Unrealistic Expectations

Comparing your spouse to someone else's partner sets them up for failure because no one is perfect. No two people, relationships, or situations are exactly alike. What works for one couple may not be suitable for another. When a spouse measures their partner against another person's actions or traits, they fail to recognize and appreciate the unique strengths and qualities that make their relationship special.

2. It Leads to Discontentment

Focusing on what another marriage has can make it easy to overlook your own blessings. When a husband or wife constantly sees what their friends or social media connections are posting, grand vacations, expensive gifts, and seemingly perfect moments, it can create the illusion that their marriage is lacking in these aspects. This discontentment can lead to resentment and emotional distance.

3. It Breeds Competition in the Marital Relationship

Marriage is a partnership, not a competition. However, when one or both spouses engage in comparison, they can begin to feel like they need to "keep up" with others rather than focusing on their journey together. This competitive mindset can cause unnecessary tension and place pressure on a marriage that was never meant to be a battleground for superiority. Instead of working together as a team, comparison pits spouses against each other in an unhealthy rivalry.

4. It Breeds a Sense of Entitlement

When comparison takes root, a spouse may begin to feel entitled to certain things simply because others have them. Instead of being grateful for what they have, they focus on what they believe they deserve. This entitlement mentality can lead to dissatisfaction, unrealistic expectations, and resentment when those expectations are not met.

5. It Invests More in the Exit Door Rather Than the Future Together

When people constantly compare their marriage to others and feel dissatisfied, they may begin to see leaving as a viable solution rather than working on their relationship. Instead of investing energy into growing together and overcoming challenges, comparison encourages the idea that "there is something better out there." This weakens commitment and can lead to avoidable breakups and divorces.

6. It Generates Too Much Negative Energy for Two People to Handle

Constant comparison adds emotional and mental strain to a marriage. When one or both partners feel like they are never good enough or their marriage always falls short, it leads to stress, insecurity, and frustration. A marriage should be a place of peace and safety, not a breeding ground for doubt and criticism.

BIBLICAL PERSPECTIVE ON AVOIDING COMPARISON

The Bible strongly warns against comparison, emphasizing contentment, gratitude, and a focus on God's plan for one's life rather than what others have.

1. Each Marriage is Unique in God's Eyes

Each one should test their actions. Then they can take pride in themselves alone, without comparing themselves to someone else (Galatians 6:4-5). Just as individuals are uniquely created by God, so are marriages. Each couple has a different journey, and what works for one may not work for another. Instead of comparing their relationship to others, couples should focus on their own growth, progress, and unique love story.

2. Contentment Leads to Peace

I have learned that in whatever situation I am, I am to be content. I know how to be brought low, and I know how to abound. In any and every circumstance, I have learned the secret of facing plenty and hunger, abundance and need (Philippians 4:11-12). Contentment is the foundation of a healthy marriage. When both spouses choose to be grateful for what they have rather than longing for what they don't, they create an environment of peace and security.

3. Comparison Distracts from the Blessings God Has Given

For where jealousy and selfish ambition exist, there will be disorder and every vile practice (James 3:16). When a spouse compares their marriage to another, they become blind to the good that already exists in their relationship. Instead of dwelling on what is lacking, couples should celebrate the blessings God has already provided.

4. Seek God's Will, Not Society's Standards

Don't just follow the way the world does things; instead, let your mind be renewed and transformed. When you do, you'll be able to understand and embrace what God's will truly is—because He is good, His plans are pleasing, and His will is perfect (Romans 12:2). The world constantly promotes an image of what marriage "should" look like, based on wealth, appearance, and social status. However, God's will for marriage is rooted in love, service, faithfulness, and unity. Couples should prioritize God's design over the world's opinions.

5. Embrace Your Spouse as God's Perfect Choice for You
He who finds a wife finds a good thing and obtains favor from the Lord (Proverbs 18:22). Instead of wishing for someone different, recognize that God has placed your spouse in your life as a blessing. Your love for them will deepen when you focus on their strengths and the positive impact they bring to your life. The key to overcoming comparison is cultivating gratitude for your unique relationship and spouse rather than measuring them against external influences.

HOW TO OVERCOME THE HABIT OF COMPARISON

1. Recognize and Acknowledge When It Happens

- Be self-aware and admit when you are falling into the trap of comparison. Ask yourself, "Why am I feeling this way?"

2. Practice Gratitude Instead of Comparison

- Shift your focus by listing three things you appreciate about your spouse whenever you are tempted to compare.

3. Limit Exposure to Social Media Triggers

- If social media fuels your dissatisfaction, take a break or unfollow pages that make you feel like your marriage is not "enough."

4. Refocus on Your Own Relationship Goals

- Instead of looking at what others have, work on building a marriage that fulfills **your** unique vision and values.

5. Pray for Contentment and a Renewed Mindset

- Ask God to help you appreciate and honor your spouse rather than longing for something different.

THE DANGER OF A TRANSACTIONAL MINDSET IN MARRIAGE

Many couples may unintentionally approach marriage with a "transactional mindset," where love and acts of service become conditional, given only in exchange for something else. This attitude can be destructive because it turns marriage into a scorekeeping institution rather than a partnership built on unconditional love. The next chapter deals with love beyond transactions in a marital relationship. In that chapter, you will understand the signs that you may view marriage as a contract instead of a covenant.

PRACTICAL WAYS TO CULTIVATE GRATITUDE IN MARRIAGE

1. Daily Appreciation Rituals

- Begin or end the day by expressing one thing you appreciate about your spouse.
- Example: "I love how you always make time for our family despite your busy schedule."

2. Gratitude Journal for Couples

- Maintain a shared journal where you write notes of appreciation to each other.
- Example: "Thank you for cooking dinner today. It made my evening easier, and I appreciate you."

3. Express Appreciation in Public and Private

- Compliment your spouse both in private and in public.
- Public affirmation reinforces admiration and builds confidence in your relationship.

4. Pray Together with Thanksgiving

- Incorporate gratitude into your prayers:

Example:

- "Lord, thank You for my spouse and our love. Help me to never take them for granted."

5. Write Love Notes or Messages

- Leave small notes of appreciation in unexpected places, such as their wallet, lunchbox, car, or pillow.
- Texting a simple "Thank you for being amazing today" can brighten their mood.

6. Acts of Service as a Form of Gratitude

- Show appreciation through actions, not just words.

- Example: If your spouse has had a tough day, offer to take over a task to ease their burden.

7. Celebrate Milestones and Everyday Moments

- Acknowledge small and big victories in each other's lives.
- Celebrating personal and marital achievements reinforces a spirit of appreciation.

8. Surprise Your Spouse with an Act of Kindness

- Do something unexpected to express gratitude, such as preparing their favorite meal or writing a heartfelt note.

EXAMPLE CONVERSATION: CULTIVATING GRATITUDE IN MARRIAGE

Scenario: A couple is struggling with feeling unappreciated in their daily routine.

Husband: *Lately, I feel like we've been so caught up in our responsibilities that we don't take time to appreciate each other.*

Wife: *I know what you mean. I feel like we're just going through the motions without really seeing each other.*

Husband: *Maybe we can start acknowledging the little things more. Like, I am very grateful that you always ensure the kids are ready in the morning. It makes my day easier.*

Wife: *I also appreciate how you always take out the trash and handle the bills. I know it's not glamorous, but it means a lot to me.*

Husband: *What if we make it a habit to say one thing we appreciate about each other every day before bed?*

Wife: *I love that idea. It'll help us focus on the good instead of just what needs to get done.*

Husband: *Exactly. I think that simple change will bring us closer."*

Wife: *Let's start tonight.*

OVERCOMING BARRIERS TO GRATITUDE

1. Breaking the Habit of Criticism

- Shift from focusing on flaws to highlighting strengths.
- Example: Instead of saying, "You never listen," try, "I appreciate when you take the time to hear me out."

2. Letting Go of Comparison

- Avoid comparing your spouse to other people or unrealistic standards.
- Gratitude is about embracing and valuing your spouse for who they are, not who they are not.

3. Recognizing Effort, Not Just Results

- Appreciate your spouse's intentions and efforts, even when things do not go perfectly.
- For example, if your spouse tries to cook dinner and it does not turn out great, appreciate the effort, not just the outcome.

4. Practicing Gratitude Even in Hard Times

- Gratitude is not conditional. It should be practiced even during tough times.
- Focusing on what is still good in the marriage helps weather difficult seasons.

ACTIVITY: GRATITUDE CHALLENGE FOR COUPLES

This exercise is designed to help couples reconnect through appreciation and thankfulness.

Step 1: Personal Reflection

- Take 5 minutes to write down five things you appreciate about your spouse.
- Reflect on how each of these qualities has positively impacted your marriage.

Step 2: Verbal Expression

- Share your list with your spouse and explain why you appreciate them.
- Take turns listening without interrupting.

Step 3: Gratitude Actions

- Choose one small act of appreciation for your spouse this week (e.g., a thoughtful note, cooking their favorite meal, or taking over a responsibility).

Step 4: Daily Gratitude Habit

- Commit to expressing one form of gratitude daily for the next 30 days.

- Keep a record of the changes you notice in your relationship.

SUMMARY

Gratitude is a powerful force that can transform a marriage from frustration and routine to one filled with joy and connection. By choosing to appreciate rather than compare, recognizing rather than expecting, and expressing love freely rather than conditionally, couples can build a marriage that thrives.

A transactional marriage operates on a basis of scorekeeping, negotiation, and conditional love. In contrast, a thriving marriage is built on grace, generosity, and commitment. If you recognize signs of a transactional mindset in your marriage, the good news is that you can shift toward a biblical, selfless love that reflects God's design. The practice of daily gratitude is an investment—one that yields long-term joy, unity, and resilience.

CHAPTER 8

LOVE BEYOND TRANSACTIONS

TRANSACTIONAL VS. TRANSFORMATIONAL LOVE

L ove is the foundation of marriage; yet, how couples define and express love can significantly determine the strength and depth of their relationship. Many relationships operate on a transactional model, where love is exchanged like a commodity, often with the expectation of getting something in return. In contrast, transformational love is rooted in selflessness, grace, and growth. It mirrors Christ's unconditional love and fosters an enduring, thriving marriage. This chapter explores the distinction between transactional and transformational love, identifies the indicators of a transactional marriage, and discusses how couples can transition toward a transformational approach that strengthens their connection and aligns with biblical principles.

WHAT IS TRANSACTIONAL LOVE?

A transactional relationship functions on an exchange-based system where love, effort, or affection is given with the expectation of something in return.

Key Characteristics

- "I will do this for you if you do that for me."
- Keeping score of who gives more or sacrifices more.
- Love is conditional, based on performance or reciprocity.
- More focused on fairness than grace.
- Emotional withdrawal when expectations are unmet.

Example

- A wife only gives her husband extra attention when he completes household chores.
- A husband only expresses affection when his wife meets his physical or emotional needs.
- A spouse withdraws kindness or intimacy as "punishment" for unmet expectations.

While fairness and mutual effort are essential in marriage, when love becomes entirely performance-based, it leads to disappointment, resentment, and emotional distance.

WHAT IS TRANSFORMATIONAL LOVE?

Transformational love is a beacon of selfless giving, grace, and personal growth. It is not about what you get but who you become through love.

Key Characteristics

- Giving without expecting immediate returns.
- Love is rooted in commitment and covenant, not convenience.

• Forgiveness and grace are practiced even when one partner falls short.

• Focused on growth, trust, and deepening intimacy.

• Mirrors Christ's love—unconditional and sacrificial.

Example

• A husband supports his wife emotionally, even when she struggles to reciprocate due to stress.

• A wife serves her husband joyfully without tracking what he has done in return.

• A couple prioritizes giving love over receiving love, trusting that a healthy relationship will naturally foster reciprocity.

Transformational love elevates a marriage from a mere partnership to a covenant that reflects God's love and character.

The Danger of a Transactional Mindset in Marriage

Many couples unintentionally approach marriage with a "transactional mindset," where love and acts of service become conditional, given only in exchange for something else. This attitude can be profoundly destructive, leading to a scorekeeping system that erodes the partnership built on unconditional love and affection.

SIGNS OF A TRANSACTIONAL MARRIAGE:

1. You Both Keep a 50/50 Mentality

A 50/50 mindset in marriage means that each spouse gives only half of the effort, expecting their partner to meet them halfway at all times. This belief can lead to frustration when one partner

perceives the other as not doing their "fair share." It's essential
to recognize that in a healthy marriage, both partners should
dedicate 100% of their effort, not just half, and that this
mindset can lead to a sense of imbalance and dissatisfaction in
the relationship.

Example: "I cleaned the house yesterday, so it's only fair that
you cook today." While sharing responsibilities is healthy,
expecting an exact trade-off for every action creates a business-
like marriage rather than a covenant relationship.

Self-examination: Do I measure my effort against my spouse's
instead of simply giving my best? Do I often find myself
keeping score in the relationship, or feeling like I'm doing more
than my fair share? These are signs of a transactional mindset
that can damage a marriage.

2. Believing You Are Doing Your Partner a Favor

Transactional spouses often feel like they are sacrificing more
than they should for their spouse, rather than loving selflessly.

Example: "I sacrificed my social life to be with you." Instead of
viewing marriage as a shared journey, they see their actions as
personal losses that deserve compensation.

Self-examination: Do I believe that my efforts in the marriage
are sacrifices rather than natural expressions of love and
commitment?

3. Enjoys Making a Deal with Your Spouse

Transactional marriages often involve **bargaining**, where spouses negotiate every aspect of their relationship.

• **Example:** "I'll go to your family gathering if you let me buy that new gadget." While compromises are essential, constantly making deals reduces emotional depth and intimacy.
• **Self-examination:** Do I often negotiate love and support instead of giving them freely?

4. Expecting a Direct Return for Every Action

In transactional relationships, spouses expect immediate reciprocity for every action they take.

• **Example:** If one spouse says, "I love you," but does not hear "I love you too" immediately, they feel hurt instead of accepting that love should be given freely.
• **Self-examination:** Do I feel unappreciated or resentful when my spouse does not immediately return a favor or affectionate gesture?

5. Expecting to Be Rewarded for Basic Acts of Love

Marriage is about serving and supporting one another, rather than seeking personal rewards.

• **Example:** "I took care of the kids today; I deserve a night out with my friends." While self-care is essential, expecting compensation for basic marital duties creates an unhealthy dynamic.
• **Self-examination:** Do I expect rewards or special treatment for doing things that should be done out of love?

6. Only Showing Appreciation When Your Spouse Meets Your Expectations

Gratitude in a transactional marriage is often conditional, given only when the other person performs well.
• **Example:** A husband only compliments his wife when she prepares his favorite meal, but never expresses appreciation for her on other days.
• **Self-examination:** Do I only express gratitude when my spouse does what I want?

7. Believing You Are Better Than the Marriage Altogether

Some people feel that they are "too good" for marriage and deserve better, which can lead to arrogance and emotional detachment.

Example: A wife constantly compares her husband to other men, believing she settled for less than she deserves.
Self-examination: Do I feel like I deserve a "better" spouse instead of focusing on growing together?

8. Only Investing as Much as You Perceive Your Partner is Investing.

This is when one or both spouses view the marriage as a Business Partnership. The relationship is more about duties and roles than emotional or spiritual connections. Every action is analyzed for its return on investment. In a healthy marriage, both partners fully commit to each other. However, in a transactional marriage, each spouse only gives as much as they feel they are receiving.

• **Example:** "If you're not putting in the effort, I won't either." This attitude turns love into a **competition** instead of a **mutual commitment.**

• **Self-examination:** Do I withhold love and effort when I feel my spouse is not giving enough?

9. You Maintain an Exit Strategy or a "Plan B."

Having an exit strategy means you mentally or emotionally prepare for separation, holding back from fully committing to your spouse and the relationship. This approach undermines trust and security in your marriage.

• **Example:** "If things don't work out, I still have my apartment and savings account separate from yours." While maintaining some financial independence can be prudent, actively preparing for separation signals conditional commitment rather than covenant loyalty.

• **Self-examination:** Do I maintain emotional or financial safeguards in case of marital failure instead of fully committing to making the marriage succeed?

10. You Believe Marriage Exists Primarily to Have Children

Seeing marriage mainly as a vehicle for procreation can lead couples to neglect emotional intimacy, companionship, and personal growth within their relationship.

• **Example:** "Our purpose is fulfilled once we have kids." While children are a blessing, a marriage founded primarily on parenting rather than partnership struggles once the children leave home, or if infertility arises.

• **Self-examination:** Have I unintentionally prioritized parenthood above nurturing my relationship with my spouse?

11. You Married Solely to Cure Your Loneliness

Choosing marriage primarily to solve loneliness sets unrealistic expectations, placing a heavy emotional burden on your spouse to provide constant companionship.

• **Example:** "I married you because I can't stand being alone." Loneliness should be addressed through personal growth and social connections, not solely through marriage. A partner cannot effectively fill emotional voids that only you and God can address.
• **Self-examination:** Did I marry primarily to fill an emotional void, or am I actively nurturing emotional and spiritual health?

12. You Keep Score of Your Contributions

Constantly tracking contributions and sacrifices in your marriage indicates a transactional mentality rather than a covenant commitment.

• **Example:** "I did this for you, so now you owe me." Love and affection become conditional, offered only when perceived fairness is maintained.
• **Self-examination:** Am I withholding affection or kindness because I feel my spouse hasn't done their "fair share"?

13. You Use Love and Affection as Rewards or Punishments

Making love, appreciation, or emotional support conditional on a spouse meeting expectations creates insecurity and emotional distance.

• **Example:** Withholding physical intimacy or kindness when upset or disappointed. This behavior reduces love to a bargaining chip rather than an unconditional expression of affection.
• **Self-examination:** Do I offer or withhold affection based solely on my spouse's performance?

14. You Practice a Tit-for-Tat Mentality

This mindset involves withholding acts of service or kindness unless your spouse reciprocates first, creating a transactional relationship rather than one based on unconditional love.

• **Example:** "If you don't help with chores, I won't support your hobbies." This type of conditional behavior breeds resentment and emotional distance.
• **Self-examination:** Do I engage in acts of service freely, or do I wait to reciprocate only when my spouse acts first?

15. You See Marriage as a Contractual Exchange of Services

Viewing marital roles strictly as defined duties, rather than as mutual acts of love and service, reduces marriage to contractual obligations.

• **Example:** "You manage the finances, and I'll handle household chores." While defined roles can foster clarity, rigid adherence without fluidity can lead to resentment, treating marriage as a transaction rather than a relationship.

• **Self-examination:** Do I focus more on roles and obligations than mutual support and shared growth?

When marriage becomes purely transactional or contractual, it loses the emotional depth, spiritual unity, and enduring commitment necessary for lasting joy and fulfillment. Viewing marriage as a sacred covenant rather than a conditional contract fosters more profound love, unconditional acceptance, and lasting intimacy.

SHIFTING FROM TRANSACTIONAL TO TRANSFORMATIONAL LOVE

Practice Grace Instead of Keeping Score

- Transformational love releases the need for fairness in every situation.
- Grace acknowledges imperfections while choosing to love anyway.

"Above all, love each other deeply, because love covers over a multitude of sins" (1 Peter 4:8).

Love Based on Covenant, Not Convenience

- Marriage is not 50/50; it is 100/100, where both spouses give their all.
- Commitment remains, even when seasons change.

"What therefore God has joined together, let no one separate" *(Mark 10:9).*

Seek to Serve Rather than to Be Served

- Shift from a self-focused mindset to a giving mindset.
- Ask: "How can I bless my spouse today?" rather than "What am I getting from this marriage?"

"The greatest among you will be your servant" *(Matthew 23:11).*

Develop Emotional and Spiritual Intimacy

- Prioritize shared experiences, prayer, and deep conversations over just fulfilling tasks.
- Example: A husband praying over his wife before bed strengthens the spiritual connection beyond physical acts of service.

Communicate Without Expecting Immediate Returns

- Express appreciation, love, and affirmation without expecting an immediate reciprocation.
- Build a habit of selfless encouragement.

"Encourage one another and build each other up" *(1 Thessalonians 5:11).*

GOD'S TRANSFORMATIONAL LOVE AS THE MODEL FOR MARRIAGE

God's love is the ultimate model for marriage, demonstrating selflessness, grace, and unwavering commitment. Throughout Scripture, God's love is transformational rather than transactional. It is given not based on merit but as an act of grace and covenantal faithfulness. If couples are to build a strong and enduring marriage, they must shift their perspective from conditional, performance-based love (transactional) to a love that reflects God's character (transformational).

GOD'S LOVE IS COVENANT-BASED, NOT CONDITIONAL

One of the foundational aspects of God's love is that it is based on covenant, not convenience. In Hosea 2:19-20, God declares, *"I will betroth you to me forever; I will betroth you in righteousness and justice, in love and compassion."* This passage highlights that God's commitment is not temporary or dependent on human faithfulness; it is steadfast and enduring.

Similarly, marriage is a covenantal relationship, not a contractual one. A contract is conditional. It remains intact only if both parties fulfill their obligations. If one fails, the contract is broken. A covenant, however, is a sacred commitment that transcends individual performance. In marriage, love should not be given or withheld based on a spouse's behavior but rather as an intentional choice to honor the covenant before God.

Practical Application in Marriage

• Instead of saying, *"I will love you as long as you meet my expectations,"* couples should declare, *"I will love you because I made a covenant to honor you and reflect Christ's love in our marriage."*

• A wife who shows kindness and serves her husband even when he forgets a critical anniversary demonstrates transformational love, mirroring God's grace toward us.

• A husband who continues to encourage and uplift his wife even when she is struggling emotionally reflects the faithfulness of God's love in difficult seasons.

CHRIST'S LOVE FOR THE CHURCH: THE BLUEPRINT FOR MARRIAGE

Ephesians 5:25-27 provides a direct comparison between Christ's love for the Church and the love husbands should have for their wives:

> "Husbands, love your wives, just as Christ loved the church and gave himself up for her to make her holy, cleansing her by the washing with water through the word."

Christ's love for the Church is self-sacrificing and purifying —He gave everything for His bride. This is transformational love in its purest form, as it focuses on the well-being, growth, and holiness of the other person rather than seeking personal gain.

Practical Application in Marriage

- Sacrificial Love: A husband who willingly sacrifices his comfort, whether by staying up late to listen to his wife's struggles or adjusting his schedule to prioritize family time, reflects Christ's love.

- Spiritual Leadership: A husband leading not through dominance but through service and encouragement embodies Jesus' role as the servant-leader of the Church.
- Purifying Love: A wife who prays for, uplifts, and encourages her husband's spiritual growth helps foster his transformation into a stronger man of God. Authentic marital leadership isn't about control but about service—leading in a way that uplifts and sanctifies the relationship.

GRACE-FILLED LOVE: LOVING BEYOND IMPERFECTIONS

God loves us not because we are perfect but because He is gracious. Romans 5:8 states, "But God demonstrates his love for us in this: While we were still sinners, Christ died for us." In the same way, marriage requires a love that extends beyond faults and failures. No spouse is perfect, and holding on to a performance-based expectation of love will lead to disappointment and resentment. Instead, a marriage built on grace and forgiveness allows both partners to grow and heal together.

Practical Application

• A husband chooses to extend grace rather than react in frustration when his wife forgets something important.
• A wife chooses to forgive rather than keep a record of wrongs when her husband makes a mistake.
• Instead of reacting with bitterness, both partners can respond with patience, humility, and the commitment to work through challenges together.
When love is freely given, rather than being treated as a reward

for good behavior, it fosters an environment of trust and emotional safety within the marriage.

LOVE THAT TRANSFORMS, NOT JUST SUSTAINS

Transformational love in marriage keeps the relationship alive and fosters its growth and flourishing. In 1 Corinthians 13:4-7, Paul describes true, godly love:

> "Love is patient; love is kind. It does not envy, it does not boast, it is not proud. It does not dishonor others, it is not self-seeking, it is not easily angered, it keeps no record of wrongs."

Each attribute is key to moving from a transactional marriage to a transformational one.

Practical Application

• **Love is patient:** When one partner struggles with personal challenges, the other does not demand immediate change; instead, they support them through the process.
• **Love keeps no record of wrongs:** Transformational love does not keep a score of past offenses but chooses to forgive and move forward.
• **Love is not self-seeking:** Instead of focusing solely on personal happiness, each spouse prioritizes serving and honoring the other.
A transactional marriage says, *"I will love you as long as you meet my needs."* A transformational marriage says, *"I will love you even when it is difficult because that is what Christ does for me."* Marriage is a human partnership and a living testimony of

God's love for His people. When couples embrace God's self-less, covenantal, grace-filled love model, they experience deep emotional intimacy, trust, and purpose.

PRACTICAL COMMITMENTS FOR A TRANSFORMATIONAL MARRIAGE

1. **Pray for Your Spouse Daily:** Seek God's help in loving and serving them selflessly.
2. **Give Without Expecting in Return:** Love freely and fully, whether through acts of service, encouragement, or emotional support.
3. **Model Grace and Forgiveness:** Extend God's mercy when your spouse falls short, just as God extends it to you.
4. **Seek to Serve, Not to Be Served:** Marriage flourishes when both partners prioritize giving over receiving.

When couples commit to living out God's transformational love, marriage becomes a place of healing, joy, and deep connection rather than a space of demands, conditions, and disappointments.

PRACTICAL SCENARIOS: TRANSACTIONAL VS. TRANSFORMATIONAL LOVE

Transactional Love

A husband and wife have been feeling disconnected. The wife feels she is doing all the household chores, while the husband feels she is not showing enough affection. Their conversation reflects a transactional mindset.

Wife: "I don't feel appreciated. I cook, clean, and take care of everything around here, but you barely acknowledge it. Why should I keep doing all this if you can't even say thank you?"

Husband: "Well, I don't feel like showing affection when I come home, and you're always nagging about something. When was the last time you just hugged me without a reason?"

Wife: "Maybe if you helped out more, I wouldn't be so frustrated all the time. I feel like I do everything, and you just expect it."

Husband: "And I feel like you only want me to help so you can check a box. Where's the love in that? Why should I put in effort when I'm just going to get criticized?"

Analysis of Transactional Love

• Both partners keep score, expecting effort in return before giving anything.
• Affection and appreciation are contingent on the other person's actions.
• Instead of focusing on connection, the conversation revolves around fairness and unmet expectations.
• This mindset can lead to resentment and emotional withdrawal.

Transformational Love

The same couple recognizes their communication issues and shifts toward a transformational approach.

Wife: "I've been feeling overwhelmed with everything at home. I know you work hard and don't want to nag, but I could use some support."

Husband: "I'm sorry you're feeling that way. I guess I've been so focused on work that I didn't realize how much you handled alone. I do appreciate everything you do."

Wife: "That means a lot. I don't need everything to be split exactly 50/50, but knowing we're a team helps."

Husband: "I want to help more, not because I feel forced, but because I love you. How about I take care of dinner twice weekly so you can have a break?"

Wife: "That would be wonderful. I will make sure to be more affectionate, I know that's something you've been missing. I want to love you in a way that makes you feel valued."

Husband: "That means a lot to me. Let's make it a goal to check in like this more often. I don't want either of us to feel like we're just trading tasks, I want us to enjoy our time together."

Analysis of Transformational Love

• Mutual understanding replaces keeping score.
• Love and effort are freely given rather than demanded.
• The couple acknowledges each other's struggles and proactively seeks solutions together.
• There is an emphasis on partnership rather than personal gain.

KEY TAKEAWAYS FROM THE SCENARIOS

• Transactional Love asks, *"What am I getting?"* while Transformational Love asks, *"How can I give?"*
• A scorekeeping mindset leads to frustration and disconnection.
• Selfless acts of love—without expecting an immediate return—build long-term trust and emotional safety.
• A covenantal perspective on marriage (rather than a contractual one) nurtures love that lasts.

Transitioning from a transactional approach to a transformational paradigm fosters an environment where love, grace, and unity thrive.

ACTIVITY: TRANSFORMATIONAL LOVE CHALLENGE

Step 1: Identify Transactional Patterns

- Reflect on areas where your marriage has become transactional.

Examples

- "Do I only express appreciation when my spouse does something for me?"

- "Do I withhold love or kindness when I'm upset?"

Step 2: Develop a Transformational Mindset

- Commit to one selfless act of love each day for the next week.

Examples

- Write a note of encouragement without expecting a response.
- Serve your spouse in a way that goes beyond duty.

Step 3: Pray for a Heart of Grace

- Ask God to help shift your perspective from one of receiving to one of giving.

- Pray together for a marriage that mirrors Christ's love.

Summary

Transactional love focuses on fairness, reciprocity, and maintaining a balance. It leads to discontentment and emotional distance. On the other hand, transformational love is rooted in grace, sacrifice, and unconditional commitment, mirroring God's covenantal love for His people. By shifting from a mindset of getting to a mindset of giving, couples experience deeper intimacy, spiritual connection, and a marriage that thrives in love rather than duty.

CHAPTER 9

INTIMACY: A SACRED ASPECT OF MARRIAGE

STRENGTHENING THE BOND BETWEEN HUSBAND AND WIFE

Intimacy is often defined too narrowly as physical closeness. However, it encompasses much more than just a sexual connection. Genuine intimacy in marriage creates a bond that includes emotional, spiritual, mental, and physical closeness. This bond fosters deep trust, understanding, and unity between spouses. Many marital struggles arise not from a lack of love but from neglecting or misunderstanding intimacy. This chapter explores the interplay of emotional and physical intimacy. It also discusses the challenges that hinder closeness. Additionally, it examines how faith, culture, and tradition shape intimacy. Ultimately, it explores the impact of intimacy on mental and spiritual well-being.

When intimacy is not actively nurtured, couples may drift apart emotionally, leading to feelings of loneliness even within the marriage. God designed intimacy as a sacred aspect of marriage to reflect oneness, vulnerability, and mutual fulfillment (Genesis 2:24). A thriving marriage prioritizes emotional and physical intimacy as they reinforce one another. Studies show that emotional closeness leads to more satisfying physical intimacy, while regular physical connection strengthens emotional bonds (Johnson & Zuccarini, 2021).

EMOTIONAL INTIMACY

Without emotional closeness, physical intimacy can feel routine, mechanical, or even forced rather than a joyful expression of love. Emotional intimacy involves vulnerability, deep conversations, shared experiences, and mutual emotional support. According to research, couples who engage in consistent emotional bonding through communication, shared activities, and affection experience greater satisfaction in their physical relationship (Fisher et al., 2018).

A husband and wife who actively listen to one another, validate their feelings, and regularly check in emotionally are more likely to feel secure, valued, and understood, naturally enhancing their physical connection. Conversely, when emotional distance creeps into a marriage, physical intimacy may suffer, often leading to frustration and misunderstanding.

Emotional intimacy is the deep bond between spouses characterized by trust, open communication, and vulnerability. It involves sharing thoughts, fears, dreams, and emotions without fear of rejection or criticism (*McNulty, 2019*). When emotional intimacy is intense, couples feel safe, valued, and deeply connected.

PHYSICAL INTIMACY

Physical intimacy includes touch, affection, and sexual connection, which play a crucial role in strengthening marital bonds. Beyond physical attraction, it fosters a sense of belonging and emotional closeness (*Worthington & Scherer, 2018*). When couples neglect physical intimacy, it often leads to feelings of rejection, resentment, or emotional detachment.

Contrary to what one may think about physical intimacy, it is not merely about sexual activity. It includes affectionate touch, hand-holding, hugging, cuddling, and any acts of closeness that reinforce emotional security. Research has shown that oxytocin, the hormone associated with bonding, is released through affectionate touch, thereby strengthening trust and connection between partners (Aron et al., 2020).

When physical intimacy is approached with love, patience, and understanding, it enhances the emotional closeness shared by a couple. However, it may lose its deeper meaning and significance when it becomes transactional, obligatory, or purely physical. Couples should strive to make physical intimacy an ongoing journey of mutual care and appreciation rather than a duty or expectation.

SPIRITUAL INTIMACY

A strong marriage is not built solely on emotions or physical attraction but rather on a shared spiritual foundation. Spiritual intimacy occurs when a couple prays, worships, studies the Word, and seeks God's guidance in their relationship. Research suggests that married couples who engage in regular spiritual activities together tend to report higher marital satisfaction, emotional stability, and greater resilience in conflict resolution (Mahoney et al., 2021).

When spiritual intimacy is present, couples tend to see their marriage as a covenant rather than just a contract. They navigate challenges with faith and trust in God rather than relying solely on human emotions. Ecclesiastes 4:12 reminds us, *"Though one may be overpowered, two can defend themselves. A cord of three strands is not quickly broken."* Spiritual intimacy strengthens most marriages against external pressures and internal conflicts.

MENTAL AND EMOTIONAL WELL-BEING

A marriage that prioritizes intimacy fosters security, trust, and emotional balance, which significantly contributes to better mental health for both partners. Research indicates that couples who experience strong emotional and physical connections report lower levels of stress, depression, and anxiety (*Emmons & McCullough, 2019*).

Intimate marriages provide a safe space where both spouses feel heard, valued, and emotionally supported, leading to increased mental resilience in navigating life's challenges. When a spouse feels emotionally distant or disconnected, mental well-being can decline, leading to increased stress, irritability, and loneliness. Therefore, prioritizing intimacy is beneficial for marriage and essential for overall mental health.

FAITH, CULTURE, AND TRADITION IN SHAPING INTIMACY

Faith plays a significant role in shaping a couple's understanding of intimacy. Religious beliefs often set moral and ethical guidelines for physical intimacy, emphasizing the sanctity of sex within marriage. The Bible teaches that sexual intimacy is a gift from God, meant to foster unity between husband and wife (1 Corinthians 7:3-5).

Faith-based marriages also emphasize serving one another selflessly, reinforcing the importance of mutual fulfillment over selfish desires. Research indicates that couples with strong religious convictions tend to have lower divorce rates and higher relationship satisfaction, likely due to their commitment to biblical principles (*Mahoney et al., 2021*).

CULTURAL VIEWS ON INTIMACY AND AFFECTION

Cultural norms greatly influence how intimacy is expressed in marriage. Some cultures encourage open displays of affection, while others maintain that intimacy should be private and reserved. For instance, in Western cultures, intimacy is often associated with emotional bonding, frequent verbal affirmation, and physical closeness.

In contrast, many African, Asian, and Middle Eastern cultures uphold more reserved expressions of affection, where public displays of love are uncommon. Understanding how culture shapes expectations about intimacy is crucial for couples, especially those from diverse backgrounds. By discussing and respecting each other's cultural beliefs, couples can find a balance that honors both their traditions and personal desires (*Xu et al., 2020*).

PRACTICAL WAYS TO STRENGTHEN EMOTIONAL AND PHYSICAL INTIMACY

Couples must actively cultivate Emotional and physical intimacy to increase their marital success. Strong marriages do not happen by accident; they require intentional effort, meaningful communication, and a deep commitment to nurturing the bond between spouses. Below are refined and strengthened strategies to help couples build a deeper connection in their marriage.

1. Engage in Daily Meaningful Conversations
Effective communication is the heartbeat of a strong emotional connection. Many couples struggle with intimacy because they fail to engage in deep, meaningful conversations beyond the day-to-day logistics of life. Emotional intimacy is

strengthened when both partners feel heard, understood, and valued.

Practical Steps

• **Check in Emotionally Every Day** – Go beyond "How was your day?" and ask meaningful questions:
  • *"What's something that made you smile today?"*
  • *"What's been on your mind lately?"*
  • *"Is there anything I can do to support you better?"*
• **Practice Active Listening**. Listen fully when your spouse speaks. Make eye contact, nod in understanding, and refrain from interrupting.
• **Be Vulnerable** – Share your fears, joys, and struggles openly. Vulnerability fosters trust and closeness in marriage.
  Why It Matters:
• Couples who engage in regular deep conversations report higher relationship satisfaction (*Gottman, 2021*).
• Meaningful dialogue prevents emotional distance and misunderstandings, strengthening emotional and physical connection.

2. Prioritize Quality Time Without Distractions

Time together should be deliberate and uninterrupted. In today's digital world, many couples spend time in the same room but remain emotionally distant due to distractions like social media, television, or work.
  Practical Steps:
• **Set a Daily or Weekly "Us" Time**—Schedule uninterrupted time together, such as morning coffee, evening walks, or weekend activities.

• **Unplug from Technology** – Turn off phones and social media notifications when spending quality time together.

• **Engage in Shared Activities** – Do something you both enjoy, such as cooking together, taking a drive, or playing a board game.

Why It Matters:

• Studies show that couples who prioritize quality time experience stronger emotional bonds and better conflict resolution (*Chapman, 2019*).

• Meaningful time together reduces stress, enhances trust, and strengthens marital unity.

3. Express Gratitude and Affirmation Regularly

Gratitude and affirmation are potent tools for emotional intimacy. Many spouses assume their partner knows they are appreciated, but unspoken appreciation often leads to feelings of neglect. Regularly expressing gratitude and affirmation creates an environment of love, warmth, and security in marriage.

Practical Steps:

• **Verbal Appreciation** – Say things like:
• *"I appreciate how hard you work for our family."*
• *"I love how thoughtful you are."*
• *"Thank you for always supporting me."*

• **Leave Notes or Send Texts** – Small written affirmations can brighten your spouse's day.

• **Praise Your Spouse in Public** – Speaking well of your partner in front of others boosts their confidence and reinforces your love for them.

Why It Matters:

• Research shows that expressing gratitude strengthens relationships by increasing trust, happiness, and satisfaction (*Emmons & McCullough, 2020*).

• Couples who frequently express appreciation report higher marital happiness and intimacy levels.

4. Pray and Worship Together

Spiritual intimacy is a powerful force that strengthens both emotional and physical closeness. When couples pray and worship together, they establish a strong spiritual foundation that draws them closer to one another and God.

Practical Steps:

• **Pray Together Daily** – Start or end the day with a simple prayer, thanking God for your marriage and seeking His guidance.

• **Read the Bible Together** – Choose devotionals on marriage, love, and intimacy.

• **Attend Church and Worship as a Couple** – Corporate worship strengthens faith and unity in marriage.

• **Serve Together** – Engaging in ministry or community service strengthens your shared purpose.

Why It Matters:

• Research shows that couples who pray together experience a more satisfying connection and greater marital stability (*Mahoney et al., 2021*).

• Spiritual intimacy creates an atmosphere of peace, trust, and emotional security, allowing couples to navigate life's challenges together.

5. Prioritize Physical Affection Beyond Sex

Physical intimacy is not just about sex—it includes all forms of touch that reinforce emotional connection. Small acts of physical affection create warmth, trust, and security in a marriage.

Practical Steps:

• **Hold Hands** – Whether walking together or sitting side by side, hand-holding fosters connection.

• **Cuddle and Hug More Often** – Physical touch releases oxytocin, the "bonding hormone," which enhances trust and reduces stress (*Fisher et al., 2018*).

• **Kiss Daily** – A genuine, lingering kiss builds anticipation, emotional connection, and intimacy.

• **Offer Non-Sexual Touch** – Give back rubs, rest your head on your spouse's shoulder, or sit close while watching a movie.

Why It Matters:

• Physical affection lowers cortisol levels (the stress hormone) and boosts emotional security (*Aron et al., 2020*).

• Regular, affectionate touch prevents emotional distance and keeps intimacy strong.

6. Make Time for Physical Intimacy and Romance

Sexual intimacy is a gift from God that strengthens the marital bond (*1 Corinthians 7:3-5*). However, many couples let work, stress, or routine life take priority over romance, leading to emotional and physical disconnect.

Practical Steps:

• **Be Intentional About Intimacy** – Do not wait for the "perfect moment." Create intentional space for intimacy in your marriage.

• **Focus on Emotional Connection First**—Emotional

closeness enhances physical intimacy. Before intimacy, engage in meaningful conversations, share laughter, and experience things together.

• **Explore What Feels Fulfilling for Both Partners** – Discuss your desires, comfort levels, and expectations openly to ensure mutual satisfaction and fulfillment.

• **Keep the Romance Alive** – Surprise your spouse with thoughtful gestures, love notes, or spontaneous date nights to maintain excitement and anticipation.

Why It Matters:

• Studies indicate that married couples who prioritize sexual intimacy report greater emotional connection and marital satisfaction (*Johnson & Zuccarini, 2021*).

• A fulfilling sex life enhances trust, emotional stability, and overall relationship quality.

THE ROLE OF SEX IN MARRIAGE: PSYCHOLOGICAL, BIBLICAL, AND BONDING PERSPECTIVES

Sex in marriage is more than just a physical act—it is a robust psychological, emotional, and spiritual connector between a husband and wife. It plays a critical role in strengthening intimacy and marital satisfaction.

Psychological Benefits

• **Reduces Stress** – Sexual intimacy releases endorphins and oxytocin, which reduce stress and increase feelings of well-being.

• **Enhances Emotional Security** – Regular physical intimacy fosters reassurance and connectedness, reducing feelings of isolation.

• **Builds Self-Esteem** – Healthy sexual intimacy

contributes to self-confidence and affirmation within the marriage.

Biblical Perspective

• **Sex as a Gift from God** – 1 Corinthians 7:3-5 reminds us that sex in marriage is a mutual responsibility and privilege, designed to bring joy and unity.

• **Reflecting God's Covenant Love** – The marital relationship mirrors the covenant between Christ and the Church (Ephesians 5:25-32).

• **Honoring Purity and Commitment** – Hebrews 13:4 emphasizes that the marriage bed should be honored, reinforcing faithfulness and exclusivity.

3. The Bonding Power of Sex

• **Enhances Emotional Closeness** – Sexual intimacy reinforces emotional security and deepens affection.

• **Fosters Commitment** – Regular physical intimacy strengthens commitment and reduces the temptation to engage in outside relationships.

• **Creates Shared Enjoyment** – A fulfilling sex life enhances marital satisfaction and builds lifelong pleasure and connection.

Couples should prioritize healthy sexual intimacy through open communication, mutual respect, and a commitment to meeting each other's needs with love and patience.

PRACTICAL EXERCISE: WEEKLY INTIMACY CHECK-IN

Each week, set aside time to ask each other:

1. Emotional Connection: What did I do this week that made you feel loved and valued?

2. Physical Closeness: How do you feel about our level of physical intimacy this week? Is there anything we should improve?

3. Spiritual Connection: Have we prayed or worshiped together? How can we grow spiritually as a couple?

4. Stress and External Pressures: Are there any external factors affecting our intimacy that we should address together?

5. Future Planning: What is one thing we can do next week to strengthen our emotional and physical bond?

This structured weekly check-in helps couples stay connected, ensuring intimacy remains a priority.

BARRIERS TO RESTORING INTIMACY

Many factors can hinder the process of rekindling intimacy in marriage. Identifying and addressing these barriers is essential for progress.

1. Unresolved Emotional Wounds

Lingering pain from past conflicts, betrayals, or disappointments creates an emotional wall that prevents intimacy from flourishing. Reconnecting becomes difficult without true healing and forgiveness (*Toussaint et al., 2021*). s ws2ej qqwwec

2. Lack of Communication

Couples who avoid discussing their needs, emotions, or concerns often experience emotional disconnection. Open communication is the foundation of intimacy, allowing both partners to feel heard and understood (*Gottman & Silver, 2022*).

3. Stress and Life Demands

Daily pressures, such as work, finances, parenting, and personal responsibilities, often overshadow intimacy. When couples become consumed by external stressors, they may unintentionally neglect each other (*McCullough et al., 2020*).

4. Differing Expectations for Intimacy

Men and women often have different expectations for emotional and physical intimacy. Misunderstandings and frustrations arise if these expectations are not communicated (*Johnson & Zuccarini, 2021*).

5. Spiritual and Cultural Influences

Religious beliefs, cultural backgrounds, and upbringing significantly impact how couples view intimacy. Some individuals may struggle to express affection due to past teachings, while others may hold unrealistic expectations influenced by external sources (*Toussaint et al., 2021*).

PRACTICAL STRATEGIES FOR RESTORING INTIMACY

Restoring intimacy requires consistent effort, intentionality, and a spirit of grace. Here are key strategies for rebuilding emotional and physical connection in marriage.

1. Prioritize Emotional Connection First

Before physical intimacy can flourish, emotional intimacy must be restored. Couples should:

- Engage in meaningful daily conversations.
- Express gratitude and appreciation regularly.
- Offer emotional support without judgment.
- Rebuild trust through honesty and openness.

2. Create an Intimacy Ritual

Couples should set aside intentional time for connection, whether through:
- Daily check-ins to share feelings and thoughts.
- Non-sexual physical touch, such as cuddling or holding hands.
- Schedule time for deeper emotional conversations.
- Special moments for shared laughter and fun activities.

3. Address Emotional Wounds Together

Healing past hurts is essential for intimacy to thrive. Couples should:
- Discuss unresolved pain safely and lovingly.
- Apologize and extend grace when needed.
- Seek counseling or pastoral support if you feel that healing is out of reach.

4. Explore Physical Intimacy with Patience

Rekindling physical intimacy should be approached with sensitivity and patience. Couples can:
- Communicate openly about desires and concerns.
- Begin with non-sexual touch, such as hugs, massages, or holding hands.
- Gradually increase physical closeness at a comfortable pace.
- Eliminate distractions to focus on each other.

5. Pray and Seek Spiritual Intimacy

Spiritual connection strengthens emotional and physical intimacy. Couples should:
- Pray together for guidance and healing.

- Engage in shared faith-based activities.
- Invite God into their marriage through intentional worship.

 Marriage thrives when both partners commit to nurturing their connection, expressing love, and seeking God's guidance.

CONCLUSION

Restoring emotional and physical intimacy in marriage is a journey that requires patience, intentionality, and faith. While external pressures and past wounds may have created distance, Couples can rekindle their intimacy through consistent effort and mutual understanding. By prioritizing emotional connection, effective communication, and physical intimacy, couples can rebuild their intimacy and strengthen their marital bond.

CHAPTER 10
FINANCIAL INTIMACY IN MARRIAGE
ALIGNING FINANCES TO STRENGTHEN YOUR BOND

F inancial intimacy is often an overlooked aspect of marriage, yet it plays a critical role in shaping trust, security, and long-term marital satisfaction. While many couples recognize the importance of physical and emotional intimacy, few actively cultivate a healthy financial relationship. Money is one of the leading causes of stress and conflict in marriage. Research indicates that financial disagreements are among the leading predictors of divorce (*Dew & Stewart, 2019*).

How couples handle finances, including how they spend, save, invest, and plan for the future, can either strengthen their relationship or become a significant source of division. God's design for marriage includes unity in all aspects, including finances. Scripture encourages stewardship, wisdom, and financial harmony in marriage:

- **Ecclesiastes 4:9-10** – *"Two are better than one, because they have a good return for their labor: If either of them falls, one can help the other up."*

- **Proverbs 21:5** – *"The plans of the diligent lead to profit as surely as haste leads to poverty."*

Financial intimacy is more than money management; it's about trust, shared goals, and financial teamwork. This chapter will examine the impact of financial intimacy on marriage, common financial conflicts, and practical strategies for fostering financial unity within marriage.

THE EFFECT OF FINANCIAL INTIMACY ON MARITAL HEALTH

Money is one of the most emotionally charged aspects of marital relationships because it represents security, independence, power, and personal values. How a couple earns, spends, saves, and manages debt directly impacts their sense of stability and emotional connection in marriage. Many marital conflicts are not caused by the amount of money a couple has but by how they handle money together.

Financial intimacy encompasses more than just managing a budget; it includes trust, shared priorities, and mutual financial stewardship. A study by Dew & Stewart (2019) found that financial conflict is one of the top predictors of divorce, even more so than disagreements about sex or household responsibilities. Financial discussions can erode trust, respect, and marital satisfaction when they lead to secrecy, control issues, or resentment.

However, when couples develop financial intimacy through honest conversations, transparency, and shared financial goals, they experience greater trust, lower stress levels, and a stronger emotional bond. Below are key ways financial intimacy influences marital health and how couples can strengthen their financial relationship.

1. FINANCIAL TRANSPARENCY BUILDS TRUST AND SECURITY

Transparency in finances is one of the strongest indicators of a healthy marital relationship. When spouses are open and honest about their income, expenses, debt, and financial goals, they foster trust and security in the marriage. However, financial secrecy, such as hidden spending, concealed bank accounts, or undisclosed debt, can significantly harm marital trust.

Signs of Financial Secrecy (Financial Infidelity)

- Making large purchases without informing your spouse.
- Maintaining secret credit cards or bank accounts.
- Lying about income, debt, or financial obligations.
- Hiding financial struggles out of embarrassment or fear.

According to Dew et al. (2020), financial infidelity can be just as damaging to a marriage as sexual infidelity because both involve broken trust and deception. When a spouse discovers hidden financial activity, it often leads to resentment, loss of security, and emotional detachment.

Practical Steps to Improve Financial Transparency

- **Share Full Financial Details** – Discuss your income, debts, assets, and spending habits openly.
- **Set Clear Financial Expectations** – Decide together how money will be managed, including savings, personal spending, and investments.

- **Use a Joint Financial Tracker**. Various Apps can help you track shared expenses transparently.

2. FINANCIAL STRESS CAN WEAKEN EMOTIONAL AND PHYSICAL INTIMACY

Financial struggles affect every aspect of a marriage, from daily interactions to long-term dreams. When money is tight, couples may experience increased anxiety, frustration, and tension, which can spill over into emotional and physical intimacy.

How Financial Stress Affects Intimacy:

Emotional Distance – Constant financial worries can distract spouses from nurturing their relationship.
Increased Conflict – Disagreements about debt, spending, and saving can lead to frequent arguments and emotional withdrawal.
Decreased Physical Intimacy – Stress about bills, loans, or financial uncertainty can reduce desire and emotional connection, making intimacy feel forced or secondary.

According to Mahoney et al. (2021), couples experiencing high levels of financial stress report lower levels of marital satisfaction and sexual intimacy. The stress of financial problems can make spouses feel irritable, exhausted, and emotionally unavailable, further widening their emotional distance.

Practical Steps to Reduce Financial Stress Together

Create a Financial Plan – Establish a budget, a debt repayment strategy, and an emergency fund to enhance financial security.

Practice Financial Prayer Together – Seek God's wisdom in financial decisions (*James 1:5*).

Have Monthly Financial Check-Ins – discuss spending, savings, and financial goals to avoid last-minute stress regularly.

3. DIFFERENT MONEY MINDSETS CAN LEAD TO POWER STRUGGLES AND MARITAL DISSATISFACTION

Every individual develops a unique relationship with money, influenced by their upbringing, personal experiences, and cultural background. For instance, consider a couple where one partner, raised in a family emphasizing saving and frugality, believes in creating a strict budget and avoiding unnecessary expenses. In contrast, the other partner grew up in a household that treated money more liberally, focusing on enjoying life and spending on experiences like travel and dining out.

When two people with differing financial perspectives get married, these differences can lead to power struggles and emotional tension over finances. As partners enter marriage, they bring their distinct perspectives on money, shaped by their familial upbringing, cultural influences, and personal histories. Although it is natural to have differing financial viewpoints, a lack of alignment in financial priorities can escalate into conflict and frustration. For example, during the wedding planning process, the frugal partner may want to limit expenditures on the ceremony.

In contrast, the spontaneous partner might be inclined to splurge on a grand event, which can lead to disagreements and stress. These differences require open communication and compromise to create a harmonious financial partnership. Below are some common money mindsets seen in marriages.

COMMON FINANCIAL MINDSETS IN MARRIAGE

Financial Mindset	Characteristics	Common Issues	Possible Solutions
Saver vs. Spender	One spouse prefers saving diligently, the other enjoys spending freely.	Frustration, resentment, conflicts over spending.	Create a balanced budget; set personal allowances.
Independent vs. Shared Finances	One partner desires separate finances; the other wants fully combined finances.	Feelings of mistrust, power struggles, insecurity.	Establish joint accounts for shared goals and keep smaller personal accounts.
Future vs. Present Oriented	One spouse prioritizes future goals; the other values immediate enjoyment.	Disagreements on priorities, unmet expectations.	Compromise on budgets that allow both savings and moderate enjoyment.
Risk Taker vs. Risk Averse	One spouse comfortable with financial risks; the other cautious and conservative.	Anxiety, tension around investments, financial security.	Set clear investment boundaries; balance risk and safety through joint planning.
Planner vs. Spontaneous	One spouse carefully plans every financial decision; the other makes spontaneous financial choices.	Financial surprises, feeling controlled or reckless.	Develop a mutual understanding and agreement on major financial decisions.

Couples who fail to understand and respect each other's financial mindset often experience miscommunication, resentment, and frustration.

HOW TO ALIGN MONEY MINDSETS

Discuss financial values early in marriage. Understand what money represents for each spouse. Find a balance between saving and enjoying your money. Create a budget that accommodates financial security and your lifestyle.

Communicate Your Money Values – Discuss honestly how

money was handled in your childhood and what it means to you today.

Please respect each other's financial perspectives, even when they differ in opinion.

Create a Financial Compromise—If one spouse wants to save aggressively while the other enjoys spending, allocate a portion of income to both priorities.

Seek Financial Counseling If Needed—A faith-based financial coach or counselor can offer objective guidance to help you align your financial goals. Create a financial plan that reflects shared goals rather than individual preferences. When couples align their financial priorities and respect each other's perspectives, they reduce financial tension and cultivate a shared vision for their future.

4. FINANCIAL PLANNING STRENGTHENS MARITAL UNITY AND FUTURE STABILITY

Couples who plan their financial future together experience stronger unity, increased trust, and greater long-term happiness. Financial planning is not just about saving money—it's about creating a shared vision for the future.

KEY AREAS OF FINANCIAL PLANNING IN MARRIAGE

Budgeting and Expense Management – Creating a joint budget helps prevent financial surprises and ensures both spouses are involved in financial decision-making.

Saving for Long-Term Goals – This is crucial for couples looking to build a secure future together. Whether buying a home, funding their children's education, or planning a comfortable retirement, establishing and working towards financial goals collectively fosters a sense of teamwork and partnership. As they navigate these crucial milestones together, couples enhance their financial stability and strengthen their relationship by promoting open communication and shared aspirations.

Offering and Generosity – Honoring God through our finances enhances spiritual unity, fosters financial discipline, and leads to overall abundance. It promotes spiritual cohesion and responsible stewardship. As stated in Luke 6:38: "Give, and it will be given to you... For with the measure you use, it will be measured back to you." This verse emphasizes that our generosity is rewarded abundantly, per our measure.

PRACTICAL STEPS TO IMPROVE FINANCIAL PLANNING

Schedule Annual Financial Goals Meetings
Meet once a year to discuss your financial aspirations for the next 5, 10, or 20 years.

Invest in Financial Literacy Together
Investing in financial literacy is essential. It helps achieve personal and communal financial health. Individuals gain insight by dedicating time to reading informative books or enrolling in financial courses. They learn about biblical principles and practical strategies for managing finances. Engaging in this journey fosters community. It encourages discussions about financial responsibility and promotes accountability. This collective exploration enhances individual understanding. It also strengthens relationships as participants share knowledge and experiences.

Pray Over Major Financial Decisions
Seeking God's guidance when faced with significant financial choices can reduce anxiety and foster a sense of peace. By incor-

porating prayer into their decision-making process, individuals can gain clarity and confidence, ultimately leading to more informed and considered choices. This practice deepens one's spiritual life and encourages thoughtful reflection on the implications of each decision, ensuring that one's actions align with one's values and faith.

COMMON FINANCIAL CONFLICTS IN MARRIAGE

Financial disagreements are among the most frequent and emotionally charged conflicts in marriage. Studies show that money disputes tend to last longer and be more intense than other marital disagreements (*Dew & Stewart, 2019*). Unlike conflicts over chores or parenting, financial disputes are often deeply rooted in personal values, fears, and long-term security concerns.

Financial issues are rarely just about dollars and cents; they touch on power dynamics, security, independence, and self-worth. If not handled properly, unresolved financial conflicts can lead to resentment, erode trust, and harm intimacy. However, when couples learn to identify, understand, and resolve financial disputes, they build financial intimacy, mutual respect, and long-term stability. Below are the most common financial conflicts in marriage, along with practical solutions to navigate them effectively.

-Disagreements Over Spending Habits

One of the most common sources of financial conflict is differences in spending habits. While one spouse may be a careful saver, the other might be a carefree spender. This dynamic can create frustration, blame, and stress, especially when financial decisions are not made together.

Common Spending Conflicts

- One spouse tends to spend impulsively, while the other prefers a more careful approach to budgeting.
- One partner believes in splurging on experiences, such as travel, dining out, and gifts, while the other values investments and savings.
- A spouse buys non-essential items without consulting their partner, which can lead to trust issues.

Solution: Create a Spending Plan Together

Set a Personal Spending Threshold – Agree on an amount each spouse can spend without prior discussion (e.g., purchases under $100).

Budget for Discretionary Spending – Allocate a set amount for each partner's expenses to allow freedom while maintaining financial stability.

Practice the 24-Hour Rule – For large purchases, agree to wait 24 hours before making the big decision. This reduces impulse spending and allows both spouses to consider the necessity of the purchase.

-Debt and Financial Burdens

Debt can place tremendous stress on a marriage, particularly if one spouse enters the relationship with significant financial obligations. Whether it's student loans, credit card debt, or car payments, differences in managing and repaying debt can lead to significant conflicts.

Common Debt-Related Conflicts:

- One spouse has a significant personal debt that the other spouse was unaware of before the marriage.
- One partner prefers aggressive debt repayment, while the other prefers minimum payments to free up cash for lifestyle expenses.
- A spouse takes on new debt (e.g., personal loans, credit cards) without informing their partner.

Solution: Develop a Debt Repayment Plan as a Team

- **Be Honest About Debt**—Discuss all financial obligations transparently before or as soon as possible after marriage.
- **Tackle Debt Together** – Decide how much of the monthly income should go toward debt repayment while maintaining savings.
- **Use the Snowball or Avalanche Method** –

- *- Snowball Method*: Pay off the smallest debts first to build momentum.
- *- Avalanche Method*: Pay off high-interest debts first to save money in the long run.

-Income Disparities and Financial Power Struggles

When incomes differ significantly, this can lead to power imbalances in the marriage. The higher-earning spouse may feel entitled to make financial decisions alone, while the lower-earning spouse may feel less valued or financially dependent.

Common Income-Related Conflicts

- The higher-earning spouse controls financial decisions, leaving the lower-earning spouse feeling excluded.
- The lower-earning spouse feels guilty or insecure about not contributing as much financially.
- One spouse expects the other to contribute equally, even if they earn significantly less.

Solution: Prioritize Financial Partnership Over Income Differences

- **Make Financial Decisions Together** – Regardless of income level, spouses should have equal say in financial planning and decision-making.
- **View Marriage as a Team** – Understand that non-financial contributions (e.g., homemaking, caregiving, emotional support) are equally valuable.
- **Create a Joint Financial Plan** – Decide how to divide expenses, save for the future, and manage investments.

-Family Obligations and External Financial Pressure

Many couples experience tension over financial responsibilities toward extended family. In some cultures, financial support from parents, siblings, or other relatives is expected, whereas in others, financial independence is emphasized.

COMMON FAMILY-RELATED CONFLICTS

- One spouse regularly sends money to the family without discussing it first.

- A family member repeatedly borrows money, straining the couple's finances.
- Cultural expectations pressure one or both spouses to support their parents or extended family financially.

Solution: Set Clear Financial Boundaries Together

- **Discuss Family Obligations Openly**. Agree on how much financial support is reasonable while ensuring your household needs are met first.
- **Create a Family Support Budget** – If family assistance is necessary, set a specific monthly amount.
- **Learn to Say No with Grace** – It's okay to support family within your means, but it should never come at the expense of your financial well-being. This will provide clear agreements and reduce misunderstandings and resentment over family-related spending.

-Different Financial Priorities and Goals

Couples often disagree on financial priorities, particularly saving, investing, or spending. These conflicts arise when one spouse prioritizes long-term financial security, while the other focuses on immediate enjoyment.

COMMON CONFLICTS OVER FINANCIAL PRIORITIES

- One spouse wants to save for a home, while the other prefers vacations and experiences.

- Disagreements on how much to save for retirement, children's education, or emergency funds.
- Conflict over when to make major purchases (e.g., buying a new car, upgrading the home, starting a business, etc.).

Solution: Align Financial Goals Through Compromise

Create a Financial Vision Together – Discuss short-term, mid-term, and long-term goals to align financial expectations.

Prioritize Savings While Enjoying Life – Strike a balance between financial security and occasional enjoyment.

Set Milestones for Major Purchases – Agree on timelines and financial readiness before making significant investments.

FINANCIAL CONFLICT IN MARRIAGE: MANAGING OBLIGATIONS TO FAMILY OVERSEAS

Financial obligations can be especially complex for couples where one or both spouses have family members living overseas. In many cultures, it is an unspoken expectation that those who have migrated or are financially stable will provide consistent financial support to parents, siblings, or extended family members back home. While this responsibility is often rooted in love, duty, and cultural values, it can also create stress, tension, and financial strain within the marriage.

These external financial responsibilities can lead to resentment, unmet expectations, and economic instability if not handled carefully. Therefore, couples must navigate this issue with wisdom, effective communication, and unity, striking a balance between their marital financial priorities and family support needs.

CHALLENGES OF SUPPORTING FAMILY OVERSEAS

Supporting family members abroad is a noble endeavor, but it can also present unique financial and relational challenges within a marriage. Some of the most common issues include:

1. Financial Strain on the Household Budget

When one or both spouses send large amounts of money overseas, it can significantly strain their household finances. If there is no agreed-upon limit or plan, financial obligations to family members can make it difficult for the couple to meet their own financial goals, such as:

- Paying off debt
- Saving for a house or children's education
- Planning for retirement
- Investing in business opportunities

The Issue: One spouse may feel they are sacrificing their financial future for the extended family's needs, while the other may feel guilty or pressured to send even more.

2. Differences in Cultural Expectations

For many immigrants or individuals from collectivist cultures (e.g., Africa, Asia, Latin America, and the Middle East), supporting one's family is not considered optional—it is often viewed as a moral and cultural obligation. However, suppose one spouse comes from a culture that values individual financial independence. In that case, they may struggle to understand why a significant amount of money is being sent back to their family member in their home country.

The Issue: If one partner sees family support as a duty, while the other sees it as an unnecessary burden, conflicts can arise about financial priorities and values.

3. Pressure from Family Members

Family members overseas may increase their financial requests over time, assuming their relative (or spouse) is financially well-off. In some cases, families may:

- Make frequent or urgent financial demands without considering the couple's economic situation.
- Expect continuous financial support as a right rather than occasional help.
- Compare financial contributions from different family members, which can lead to guilt-tripping or emotional manipulation.
- The Issue: One spouse may feel torn between obligations to their spouse and their extended family, leading to guilt, stress, and emotional burnout.

4. Lack of Boundaries and Transparency

If financial support to family members is not openly discussed or agreed upon, it can lead to hidden transactions, financial secrecy, and a breakdown of trust in marriage.

The Issue: The spouse providing financial support may feel defensive, while the other may feel betrayed or unheard.

PRACTICAL SOLUTIONS FOR MANAGING OVERSEAS FINANCIAL SUPPORT AS A COUPLE

While supporting family members overseas is essential, it should not come at the cost of the couple's financial stability or marital harmony. Below are ways to navigate this issue wisely and effectively:

1. Have an Honest and Transparent Financial Discussion

- The first step is open communication. Both spouses must discuss the following:
- How much money is currently being sent overseas?
- How often is financial assistance given?
- Who is being supported, and whether this support is long-term or temporary?
- How does it impact the household budget and future financial goals?

Key Action: List all current financial commitments and determine if any adjustments are necessary.

2. Set Clear Boundaries on Financial Support

Couples must establish firm but loving boundaries regarding financial assistance for extended families.

Solutions

- Determine a Set Monthly or Annual Budget for family assistance.
- Agree on Emergency Help Only—Limit assistance

to unexpected crises (e.g., medical emergencies)
instead of routine support.
- Communicate Boundaries to Family Members –
Politely but firmly let them know:
- *"We are happy to help within our means, but we also
have responsibilities at home."*
- *"We will assist when possible, but cannot commit to
continuous financial support."*

Key Action: Craft these agreements to ensure both spouses
feel accountable and aligned.

3. Prioritize the Financial Stability of Your Household

A marriage cannot thrive if its financial foundation is unstable.
Before sending large sums of money overseas, couples should
first:

- Eliminate personal debt, including credit cards,
loans, and car payments.
- Build an emergency savings fund for at least three
to six months of expenses.
- Secure investments and retirement funds for long-
term financial security.

Key Action: If finances are tight, agree that family support
should not come from emergency savings or debt.

4. Find Alternative Ways to Support Family

Financial help is not the only way to care for loved ones
overseas. Some families become overly dependent on remit-
tances rather than developing sustainable income sources.

Alternative Ways to Help:

- Invest in their self-sufficiency by funding a small business or sponsoring job training.
- Provide financial education to help family members manage their money wisely.
- Support in non-financial ways (e.g., helping them apply for scholarships, networking for job opportunities).

Key Action: Instead of creating financial dependency, focus on empowerment and sustainability.

5. Make Financial Decisions as a Team

Financial unity is crucial in marriage. Neither spouse should make significant financial commitments without the other's agreement.

Solutions

- Create a Financial Agreement – Decide how much each spouse can allocate for family support.
- Use a Joint Financial App—Good, highly rated Apps can help track expenses and inform both partners.
- Set a Review Date – Regularly reassess financial commitments and adjust as needed.
- Key Action: Treat financial decisions as a partnership rather than an individual obligation.

BIBLICAL AND ETHICAL PERSPECTIVE ON SUPPORTING FAMILY

God calls us to honor our families, but not at the expense of our marriage.

Balance Giving with Responsibility
- *1 Timothy 5:8 – "Anyone who does not provide for their relatives, and especially for their household, has denied the faith and is worse than an unbeliever."* While we are called to help family, our first responsibility is to our immediate household.

Give with a Cheerful Heart, Not Obligation
- *2 Corinthians 9:7 – "Each of you should give what you have decided in your heart to give, not reluctantly or under compulsion."* Giving should be intentional and joyful, not forced or driven by guilt.

Practice Wisdom in Financial Giving
- *Proverbs 21:5 – "The plans of the diligent lead to profit as surely as haste leads to poverty."* Wise financial planning ensures both family and marriage remain stable.

STRENGTHENING YOUR MARRIAGE WHILE SUPPORTING FAMILY OVERSEAS

Navigating financial support from family overseas requires wisdom, balance, and teamwork. Couples must establish clear financial boundaries, prioritize their household stability, and find sustainable ways to help loved ones without compromising their future.

Rather than allowing this issue to create division or stress, couples should view it as an opportunity for teamwork and growth. When financial decisions are made together with transparency and love, they can strengthen trust, unity, and financial peace within a marriage.

Practical Steps to Build Financial Intimacy in Marriage

1. Create a Shared Financial Vision

Financial unity begins with defining shared financial goals. Discuss where you want to be financially in 5, 10, or 20 years and create a plan to achieve those goals together.

Action Steps

- Set short-term, mid-term, and long-term financial goals.
- Decide on priorities, such as saving for a home, investing, or giving to charity.
- Align financial goals with God's principles of stewardship (Proverbs 3:9).

2. Budgeting as a Team

A well-structured budget helps prevent financial stress and fosters effective teamwork. Instead of viewing budgeting as restrictive, consider it a tool for achieving financial freedom.

Action Steps

- Use a budgeting app or spreadsheet to track income and expenses.
- Have monthly financial check-ins to discuss spending, saving, and adjustments.
- Make financial decisions together, ensuring that both spouses have input.

3. Tithing and Giving Together

When we give generously, we acknowledge that everything we have is a gift from God and we foster a sense of trust and dependence on His provision. This act of giving can also strengthen our relationship with others as we support causes that align with our values and bring blessings to our community.

Action Steps

- Set aside a percentage of income for offering or tithing, making it a consistent practice that reflects our commitment and trust in God's provision.
- Find charitable causes you both care about and give together, creating shared values and a unified purpose in serving others.

4. Build Financial Security Together

Financial security reduces stress, prevents uncertainty, and builds trust.

Action Steps

- Create an emergency fund with at least 3-6 months' expenses.
- Invest in retirement savings to secure your future.
- Ensure financial protection through life insurance, wills, and estate planning.

CONCLUSION

Every marriage will encounter financial disagreements, but how couples handle them determines whether those conflicts strengthen or weaken their bond. By practicing financial transparency, setting boundaries, aligning spending habits, and making joint financial decisions, couples can build a healthy, financially intimate marriage.

Financial intimacy is essential for marital stability, trust, and unity. A strong financial relationship requires open communication, shared goals, and teamwork in managing finances. When couples prioritize financial transparency, budget as a team, and align their finances with biblical principles, they can create a secure, God-honoring, and financially healthy marriage.

Rather than allowing money to be a source of division, couples should use financial planning to build trust, teamwork, and a shared vision for the future. With open communication, mutual respect, and wise financial stewardship, financial conflicts can be transformed into opportunities for more profound marital unity.

CHAPTER 11

RESTORING INTIMACY AFTER HURT 1

THE JOURNEY OF REBUILDING INTIMACY

Restoring intimacy after trust has been broken is a delicate and intentional process. While forgiveness lays the foundation for healing, emotional and physical intimacy must be rebuilt through consistent effort, vulnerability, and patience. Many couples assume closeness will naturally return once an apology is made and trust is restored. However, intimacy thrives on emotional security, mutual understanding, and a willingness to connect meaningfully.

Healing intimacy is a journey, not a destination. It requires understanding different forms of closeness, recognizing barriers, and taking proactive steps to rebuild the connection. This chapter examines the dimensions of intimacy, common obstacles to rebuilding it, and practical strategies to foster a thriving, connected marriage following hurt.

UNDERSTANDING THE DIFFERENT DIMENSIONS OF INTIMACY RESTORATION

1. Emotional Intimacy

Emotional intimacy is the foundation of any strong marriage. It involves vulnerability, deep conversations, and mutual support. However, a breach of trust may compromise emotional safety, making it difficult to open up and share feelings.

Example: After James hid his financial struggles from his wife, Sarah found it difficult to trust his words. Every financial discussion triggered suspicion. Through structured daily check-ins and reassurance, they slowly rebuilt their emotional connection.

Ways to Rebuild Emotional Intimacy

- Engage in daily heart-to-heart conversations without distractions.
- Express appreciation and validation regularly.
- Set aside time for intentional quality time and shared experiences.

2. Physical Intimacy

Physical intimacy extends beyond sex—it includes affection such as holding hands, hugging, cuddling, and kissing. Many couples struggle with rekindling physical intimacy, especially when emotional wounds are still healing.

Example: Maria struggled to reconnect physically with her husband, David, after his past emotional neglect. They began with small non-sexual gestures, such as holding hands and hugging, which gradually restored their comfort level.

Steps to Rekindle Physical Closeness

- Begin with non-sexual touch, such as hugs, sitting close together, or gentle forehead kisses.
- Engage in intentional affectionate gestures, such as surprise love notes or playful touches.
- Communicate openly about comfort levels and desires.

3. Spiritual Intimacy

A shared spiritual foundation strengthens emotional and physical bonds in marriage. When couples seek God together, they create a sense of unity that reinforces trust and connection.

Example: After a season of emotional disconnection, John and Rachel committed to praying together every night. Initially, it felt awkward, but over time, these moments deepened their bond and restored their faith in each other.

Ways to Strengthen Spiritual Intimacy

- Pray together daily, inviting God's healing into your marriage.
- Read Bible verses on love and restoration together (e.g., 1 Corinthians 13).
- Engage in faith-based activities as a couple, such as worship or service projects.

4. Psychological Intimacy

Psychological intimacy involves understanding each other's

thought processes, fears, and perspectives. Without this, couples may feel emotionally distant even if they spend time together.

Example: Lisa struggled with postpartum depression, causing emotional withdrawal from her husband, Mark. Mark learned how to support Lisa without pressure through patience and intentional discussions.

Ways to Strengthen Psychological Intimacy

- Have deeper conversations about life, fears, and dreams.
- Support each other's mental well-being without judgment.
- Practice active listening—seek to understand rather than to respond.

Barriers to Restoring Intimacy

i. **Lingering Emotional Pain:** Even after forgiveness, wounds can take time to heal.
ii. **Differing Expectations:** One spouse may be ready to reconnect while the other still feels hesitant.
iii. **Fear of Being Hurt Again:** A betrayed spouse may struggle with vulnerability.
iv. **Guilt and Shame:** The offending spouse may feel unworthy of love or affection.
v. **Lack of Emotional Connection:** Physical intimacy without emotional security may feel forced.

Solution

Both partners must communicate openly, set realistic expectations, and take intentional steps toward reconnection at a comfortable pace.

PRACTICAL STRATEGIES FOR REKINDLING INTIMACY

1. Rebuild Emotional Safety First

- Set daily check-ins to discuss feelings and progress.
- Use affirmations and encouragement to reassure your spouse.
- Create a safe space for open communication, free from judgment and criticism.

2. Strengthen Physical Closeness Gradually

- Begin with non-sexual affection, such as holding hands, forehead kisses, or back rubs.
- Introduce intentional touch. A slight, everyday gesture of warmth is grand.
- Engage in shared activities that encourage physical closeness.

3. Cultivate Spiritual Intimacy

- Pray together for guidance, healing, and strength.
- Meditate on scriptures about love and restoration (Ephesians 5:25-33).
- Attend faith-based marriage workshops or small groups.

4. Implement the "Reconnection Plan."

This structured approach helps couples rebuild trust and intimacy in a step-by-step manner, allowing them to progress at their own pace.

Here is the reconnection plan. Follow it step by step as much as possible.

Step 1: Emotional Connection

- Set aside a daily or weekly time to discuss your emotions and fears.
- Express appreciation for your spouse's effort to rebuild trust.

Step 2: Physical Closeness Without Pressure

- Start with simple gestures, such as cuddling or holding hands.
- Create an atmosphere of safety and respect, allowing each other to maintain their pace.

Step 3: Spiritual Reconnection

- Commit to praying together and seeking God's guidance.
- Share faith-building activities, such as devotionals or worship music.

Step 4: Gradual Physical Intimacy

- Be open about expectations, desires, and boundaries.
- Approach intimacy as an expression of love, not just a physical act.

Reflection Questions

Take time to reflect on these questions individually and discuss them as a couple:

1. What emotions still need to be addressed before we can reconnect fully?
2. What fears do I have about restoring intimacy, and how can we work through them together?
3. How can we improve our emotional, physical, and spiritual connection?
4. What small steps can we take this week to nurture closeness?
5. How can we invite God into the process of rebuilding our intimacy?

CASE STUDY 1: REKINDLING AFFECTION AFTER BETRAYAL

Chris and Emily had been married for ten years when Emily discovered that Chris had developed an emotional affair with a coworker. Though no physical betrayal had occurred, Emily felt deeply hurt by the secrecy and emotional investment Chris had given to someone else. She struggled with trust and found it difficult to be emotionally or physically affectionate toward him.

Chris, remorseful and committed to rebuilding their relationship, wanted to reconnect quickly, but Emily felt emotionally guarded. She feared that physical intimacy would feel forced or that she would betray her own emotions by pretending everything was fine.

Steps Toward Restoration

1. **Emotional Healing First** – With the help of a marriage counselor, Chris and Emily established emotional safety before physical reconnection. They dedicated time to open, judgment-free conversations where Emily could express her hurt, and Chris could reaffirm his commitment to their marriage.

2. **Daily Affirmations & Reassurance** – Chris wrote Emily handwritten notes, reminding her of his love and appreciation, which helped rebuild her emotional security.

3. **Gradual Physical Reconnection** – Instead of rushing into intimacy, they reintroduced physical affection through non-sexual touch, such as holding hands, forehead kisses, and cuddling while watching TV. Over time, Emily felt safe enough to re-establish their physical connection.

Key Takeaway

Trust and emotional security must come first. Once emotional intimacy is restored, physical connection becomes a natural expression of love rather than an obligation.

CASE STUDY 2: OVERCOMING EMOTIONAL DISCONNECTION IN A STRESSFUL SEASON

Ryan and Jessica had been married for five years when Jessica began to feel emotionally disconnected from Ryan. Work stress, family responsibilities, and the challenges of raising a young child left them exhausted and distant. While they were not fighting, they rarely had deep conversations or moments of affection, making their relationship feel more like roommates than romantic partners. Jessica feared that the emotional distance would turn into long-term disconnection. Overwhelmed by work pressure, Ryan hadn't realized how distant he had become.

Steps Toward Restoration

1. **Intentional Quality Time** – They scheduled a weekly "Us Time"—a dedicated period without distractions to reconnect emotionally. These evenings included deep conversations, reminiscing about their early days, and discussing dreams for the future.

2. **The Gratitude Journal** – Jessica and Ryan began writing down one thing they appreciated about each other every day. This helped them shift their focus from frustrations to gratitude, reigniting warmth and connection.

3. **Non-Verbal Affection** – They made a rule to hug for at least 30 seconds daily to promote bonding and relaxation. This simple gesture helped them reconnect without needing to force words.

Key Takeaway

Emotional distance often comes from stress, not a lack of love. Small, intentional steps can reignite closeness without pressure.

CASE STUDY 3: RESTORING SPIRITUAL INTIMACY AS A PATH TO RECONNECTION

Michael and Sophia had always been strong in their faith, but over time, they had stopped praying together and engaging in spiritual activities as a couple. Michael felt spiritually drained, and Sophia noticed that their marriage lacked depth. They weren't arguing, but their relationship felt routine and uninspired.

Steps Toward Restoration

1. **Reintroducing Prayer as a Couple** – They began praying

together before bed, using prayer not just for their own needs but also to thank God for their relationship.

2. **Faith-Based Connection**—To realign their spiritual and emotional connection, they began reading a devotional together each morning and attended a faith-based marriage workshop.

3. **Acts of Service for One Another** – Inspired by biblical teachings on love and servanthood, they sought out small ways to serve one another daily. Sophia began making Michael's favorite coffee in the mornings, and Michael started writing encouraging scripture-based notes for Sophia.

Key Takeaway
Spiritual intimacy fosters deeper emotional and physical connections. Engaging in faith-based activities together helps deepen the marriage bond.

Restoring Intimacy in Long-Distance Marriages

Rebuilding intimacy in a long-distance marriage presents unique challenges. Geographic separation can create emotional distance due to factors such as military service, career demands, or family obligations. However, couples can still maintain strong emotional, physical, and spiritual connections with intentionality and effort.

CHALLENGES OF LONG-DISTANCE MARRIAGES

Emotional disconnect – A lack of physical presence can make emotional support more challenging.

Miscommunication – Without nonverbal cues, messages can be misinterpreted.

Decreased physical intimacy – The absence of touch can create feelings of longing or detachment.

Trust issues – Distance can sometimes heighten insecurities or fears of disconnection.

STRATEGIES FOR REBUILDING EMOTIONAL INTIMACY FROM A DISTANCE

1. Prioritize Consistent, Meaningful Communication

Long-distance couples must be intentional about their communication to prevent emotional drift.

- Set daily or weekly "connection calls" where partners give each other full attention.
- Use video calls frequently to maintain visual and emotional closeness. Seeing facial expressions and reactions helps prevent misinterpretations.
- Send voice messages—hearing your spouse's tone adds warmth to the conversation.

Pro Tip

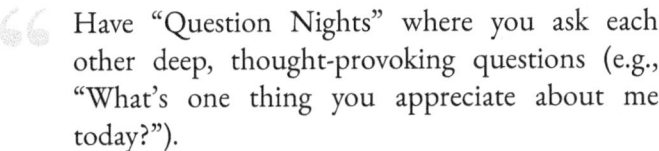

Have "Question Nights" where you ask each other deep, thought-provoking questions (e.g., "What's one thing you appreciate about me today?").

2. Maintain Physical Intimacy Through Creative Means

While physical closeness is limited in long-distance marriages, couples can still nurture a sense of closeness.

- Send surprise care packages with handwritten love letters, favorite snacks, or meaningful gifts.
- Plan virtual date nights—watch a movie together, cook the same meal, or play an online game.
- Wear meaningful jewelry that reminds you of your spouse's presence.

Pro Tip

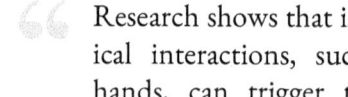 Research shows that imagining positive past physical interactions, such as hugging or holding hands, can trigger the release of oxytocin, a hormone associated with bonding and emotional attachment.

3. Strengthen Spiritual Intimacy Despite the Distance

- Couples can keep God at the center of their marriage even when apart.
- Pray together over the phone or through messages.
- Read the same devotional passage or scripture daily and share your reflections on it.
- Join together in prayer for a specific request to foster spiritual unity.

Pro Tip

 Record a prayer or blessing and send it to your spouse. Hearing your voice in prayer can be deeply reassuring.

THE RECONNECTION PLAN FOR LONG-DISTANCE COUPLES

Step 1: Schedule Time for Reconnection

- Plan reunions ahead of time so both partners can look forward to something.
- Have realistic expectations—adjusting to being together again takes time.

Step 2: Rebuild Physical Intimacy Gradually

- Ease back into affection with small gestures first.
- Focus on emotional connection first before jumping into physical intimacy.

Step 3: Strengthen Emotional and Spiritual Bonding

- Continue the habits you built while apart (e.g., deep conversations, prayer, gratitude).
- Use the time together wisely—create memories rather than spending time on devices.

Rebuilding intimacy after trust has been broken—or in the face of physical distance—requires intentionality, patience, and a sense of grace. While challenges are inevitable, couples who prioritize emotional, physical, and spiritual connection can emerge stronger.

Encouragement

Though one may be overpowered, two can defend

*themselves. A cord of three strands is not
quickly broken (Ecclesiastes 4:12).*

Here's an expanded section on intimacy-building exercises
specifically for long-distance couples, incorporating emotional,
physical, and spiritual connection.

INTIMACY-BUILDING EXERCISES FOR LONG-DISTANCE COUPLES

Even in a long-distance marriage, intimacy can thrive through
intentional habits and creativity. The following exercises will
help rekindle emotional closeness, maintain a sense of physical
connection, and deepen spiritual intimacy.

1. The Daily Connection Check-In (For Emotional Intimacy)

Goal: Stay emotionally attuned to each other's feelings and
experiences.

How It Works:
Start and end the day with a meaningful check-in. This can be
as simple as:

- "How are you feeling today?"
- "What was the best/worst part of your day?"
- "Is there anything you'd like to share on your
  mind?"
- Use voice or video messages for added warmth
  instead of just texts.
- Keep the conversation intentional—don't just
  discuss logistics (bills, kids, schedules).

Why It Works:

- Helps prevent emotional distance.
- Encourages openness and vulnerability.
- Ensures both partners feel heard and supported.

2. Love Notes Across the Distance (For Emotional & Physical Connection)

Goal: Bring back the romance and make your spouse feel cherished.

How It Works:

- Write handwritten love letters and mail them. There's something special about a physical note rather than just texts.
- Leave surprise messages in their luggage, wallet, or car before they leave.
- Create a digital memory book with favorite texts, photos, and shared experiences.

Bonus
Send a scented item, such as a favorite T-shirt, hoodie, or scarf, that has been sprayed with your perfume or cologne. The smell of your spray is deeply tied to memory and emotions!

Why It Works

- Increases a sense of closeness and affection.
- Keeps romance alive despite the distance.
- Creates sentimental keepsakes that reinforce commitment.

3. Virtual Date Nights (For Emotional & Relational Intimacy)

Goal: Maintain a sense of quality time and fun despite the physical separation.

How It Works

- Movie Night - Choose a film, sync up your screens, and watch together via video call.
- Cook Together - Choose the same recipe and cook together over video chat.
- Online Games - Play relationship-building games like "Would You Rather" or "20 Questions."
- Deep Dive Conversations:

Use conversation starters like

- "What's a dream you've never told me about?"
- "What's something you admire about me that I might not realize?"

<u>Pro Tip</u>

 Plan special occasion virtual dates—celebrate anniversaries, birthdays, and milestones creatively!

Why It Works

- Maintains a sense of togetherness and fun.
- Breaks up monotony and keeps things fresh.
- Strengthens friendship and emotional intimacy.

4. Prayer & Devotion Together (For Spiritual Intimacy)

Goal: Stay spiritually united and strengthen faith as a couple.

How It Works

- Schedule a shared prayer time. Even five minutes a day can build a connection.
- Choose a Bible passage or devotional to read separately, then discuss.
- Fast together for a shared purpose—praying for your marriage, future, or challenges.
- Send scripture-based encouragement messages throughout the day.

Pro Tip

 Record a short prayer or blessing and send it as an audio message for your spouse to listen to when they wake up or before bed.

Why It Works

- Reinforces the foundation of faith in your marriage.
- Provides peace, comfort, and guidance.
- Creates a sense of unity even when apart.

5. The 30-Day Connection Challenge (For Emotional & Physical Closeness)

Goal: Reignite intimacy by consistently engaging in small but meaningful acts of love.

How It Works

Each day, do one small act of emotional, spiritual, or romantic connection.

- Day 1 - Send a voice memo saying, "I love and appreciate you because..."
- Day 2 - Pray together over the phone.
- Day 3 - Write and send a heartfelt email.
- Day 4 - Plan your next reunion and discuss what you would like to do.
- Day 5 - Share a favorite memory from when you were last together. Continue with daily intentional actions that keep your marriage a priority.

Why It Works

- Prevents drifting apart.
- Encourages daily investment in the relationship.
- Keeps the excitement alive.

6. Sensory Connection Exercise (For Physical & Emotional Intimacy)

Goal: Maintain a feeling of physical closeness despite the distance.

How It Works

- Use scent, touch, and sound to stay connected
- Listen to a playlist of songs that remind you of each other.
- Send a scarf or hoodie with your scent on it.

- Watch videos of shared experiences, like wedding videos, vacations, or past date nights.
- Sync your schedules occasionally, if time zones allow, wake up and have coffee "together" over video.

Pro Tip

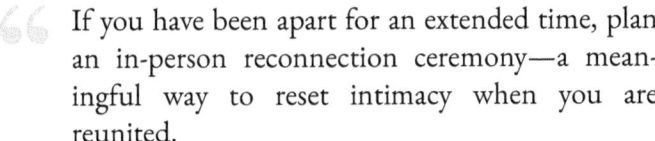

If you have been apart for an extended time, plan an in-person reconnection ceremony—a meaningful way to reset intimacy when you are reunited.

Why It Works:

- Helps bridge the physical separation gap.
- Keeps the emotional and physical connection alive.
- Creates sensory reminders of love and affection.

7. 'The Future Dream List' (For Long-Term Emotional & Relational Intimacy)

Goal: Remain focused on your future vision and build something to anticipate.

How It Works

- Write down long-term goals for your marriage (e.g., dream vacation, home projects, spiritual goals).
- Create a bucket list together—things you'll do once you're back in the same place.
- Plan intentional reunions—precise reunion dates reduce anxiety and build anticipation.

Why It Works

- Prevents hopelessness in long-distance relationships.
- Strengthens commitment by reinforcing shared dreams.
- Keeps excitement alive in the relationship.

Final Thoughts: Keeping the Connection Alive

A long-distance marriage does not mean that emotional or physical distance has to grow. Intimacy can be cultivated creatively and intentionally to keep the relationship thriving.

Final Encouragement

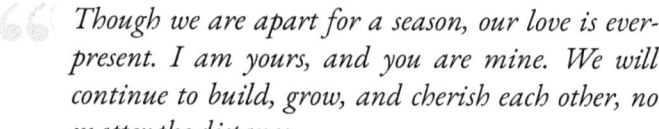

Though we are apart for a season, our love is ever-present. I am yours, and you are mine. We will continue to build, grow, and cherish each other, no matter the distance.

RESTORING INTIMACY AFTER HURT 2

REKINDLING INTIMACY AFTER A LONG SEPARATION

Rekindling intimacy after a prolonged separation can be a delicate and emotional journey for couples. Whether the distance was due to immigration, military deployments, demanding work assignments, or other extended periods apart, it often leaves a lasting impact on both individuals. Time apart may bring about personal growth and changes, making the reconnection process both challenging and rewarding. Restoring emotional, physical, and spiritual bonds requires intentional effort, patience, and compassion. Here are some practical and heartfelt exercises designed to help couples rebuild and deepen their intimacy after such a transformative period.

1. THE REUNION EXPECTATIONS TALK (FOR EMOTIONAL & RELATIONAL INTIMACY)

Goal: Align expectations before reuniting to prevent misunderstandings and unmet needs.

How It Works
Before returning home, schedule a deep conversation to discuss your feelings and emotions.

Topics to discuss

- What are you most excited about upon reuniting?
- Are there any concerns or fears about transitioning back to being together?
- What are some things that have changed in your routine while you have been apart?
- How can we best support each other during this transition?
- Listen actively and without judgment. The goal is to approach the reunion with understanding, rather than assumptions.

<u>Pro Tip</u>

 Before reuniting, write each other a letter about what you missed most. This will create warmth and reassurance.

Why It Works

- Prevents tension or unmet expectations.
- Creates an emotionally safe space for open communication.
- Helps both partners feel seen and understood.

2. THE 48-HOUR RECONNECTION ZONE (FOR PHYSICAL & EMOTIONAL INTIMACY)

Goal: Prioritize undistracted quality time during the first two days together.

How It Works
Set aside dedicated time (ideally 48 hours) for just the two of you, no work distractions, no social obligations, and limited technology.

Engage in meaningful but straightforward activities:

- Have a slow, uninterrupted dinner.
- Take a walk together and talk about personal updates.
- Spend time holding hands, hugging, and re-establishing physical closeness.

Do not rush into 'normal' routines. Let the first few days be about rekindling your bond, not catching up on chores or responsibilities.

Pro Tip

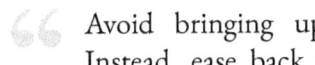 Avoid bringing up major issues immediately. Instead, ease back into deep conversations over time.

Why It Works

- Prevents feeling overwhelmed by responsibilities too quickly.
- Helps both partners relax and fully embrace the reunion.
- Allows physical and emotional intimacy to rekindle naturally.

3. THE SLOW REBUILD (FOR PHYSICAL INTIMACY & TRUST)

Goal: Ease back into physical closeness rather than expecting instant chemistry.

How It Works

- Start with non-sexual physical affection.
- Hold hands often.
- Give back rubs or sit close while watching a movie.
- Cuddle without expectations.

Have open conversations about comfort levels and desires. Long separations sometimes bring hesitation, so checking in on emotional and physical comfort is key.

Pro Tip

 If either partner feels disconnected, schedule a "touch practice" session. Spend time just exploring gentle touch, without rushing into sex —this builds safety and anticipation.

Why It Works

- Removes pressure to "jump back in" too quickly.
- Helps restore trust and safety in physical connection.
- Creates an intimate atmosphere without stress.

4. THE NEW NORMAL CHECK-IN (FOR EMOTIONAL & RELATIONAL GROWTH)

Goal: Adjust to post-reunion life and ensure both partners feel supported.

How It Works
Two weeks after reuniting, set aside time for a 'New Normal Check-In.'

Topics to discuss

- How has the adjustment back to everyday life been?
- Are there any emotional or logistical challenges in the transition?
- What new habits or changes have we noticed in each other?
- How can we maintain an intense intimacy moving forward?

Revisit the conversation every few months to maintain emotional closeness and intimacy.

Pro Tip

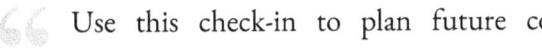 Use this check-in to plan future connection

points, such as date nights, getaways, or new traditions.

Why It Works

- Strengthens long-term emotional intimacy.
- Helps identify any struggles early before they create distance.
- Reinforces teamwork as you adjust to life together again.

5. REBUILDING SHARED RITUALS (FOR SPIRITUAL, EMOTIONAL, & PHYSICAL INTIMACY)

Goal: Restore relationship routines and traditions that may have faded during separation.

How It Works
Identify rituals that bring you closer, and reintroduce them.

Examples:

- Praying together before bed.
- Taking Sunday walks after church.
- Setting aside 15 minutes of pillow talk each night.
- Cooking a special meal together weekly.

If your old routines no longer fit your current season, create new ones.

<u>Pro Tip</u>

Create a list of 3-5 rituals to either reintroduce or start anew within the first month of being together.

Why It Works

- Creates consistency in emotional bonding.
- Reinforces the couple's unique connection and traditions.
- Helps transition smoothly into everyday life together.

6. THE MEMORY LANE DATE (FOR EMOTIONAL & RELATIONAL INTIMACY)

Goal: Strengthen emotional reconnection by reliving cherished memories.

How It Works

- Plan a date or evening centered on reminiscing about activities or things that have helped you in the past.
- Watch old videos or look through past photos.
- Visit a meaningful place (first date spot, favorite restaurant, etc.).
- Recreate a memorable moment from the past (a favorite trip, meal, or event).

Share reflections on why you love each other

- "One of my favorite memories with you is..."
- "I love the way you..."

- "I'm grateful for how you supported me during..."

<u>Pro Tip</u>

 End the date by writing each other a new love note or future vision letter.

Why It Works

- Rekindles appreciation and emotional closeness.
- Reinforces positive memories rather than dwelling on past difficulties.
- Strengthens the emotional foundation for moving forward.

7. INTIMACY RECOMMITMENT NIGHT (FOR SPIRITUAL, EMOTIONAL & PHYSICAL CLOSENESS)

Goal: Make a fresh commitment to deepen intimacy and unity after time apart.

How It Works
Set up a special evening dedicated to reconnecting on all levels

- Begin with a shared prayer or devotional.
- Read scriptures about love, unity, and renewal (Song of Solomon, 1 Corinthians 13).
- Have an honest conversation about needs, desires, and emotional well-being.
- Express gratitude through verbal affirmations or written notes.

- End the night with intentional, affectionate time together (non-sexual or sexual, depending on comfort level).

<u>Pro Tip</u>

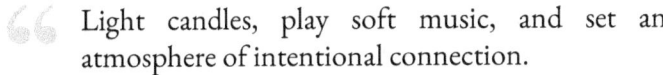

Light candles, play soft music, and set an atmosphere of intentional connection.

Why It Works

- Reinforces spiritual and emotional unity.
- Creates space for deep reflection and appreciation.
- Helps transition from distance back into complete intimacy.

Final Thoughts

Rebuilding Takes Time, But It's Worth It. Reuniting after a long separation can feel overwhelming, but with patience, intentionality, and love, intimacy can be restored stronger than before.

Encouragement

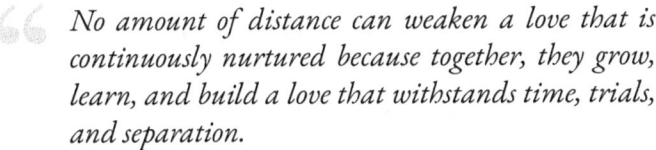

No amount of distance can weaken a love that is continuously nurtured because together, they grow, learn, and build a love that withstands time, trials, and separation.

NAVIGATING INTIMACY STRUGGLES AFTER A LONG SEPARATION

Reconnecting after a long time apart can be joyful, but it can also be complicated. While there's excitement, many couples face unexpected challenges that lead to emotional withdrawal due to mismatched expectations about physical intimacy. Recognizing and addressing these issues early can help prevent deeper disconnection and ensure that intimacy is restored healthily and satisfyingly.

1. EMOTIONAL WITHDRAWAL: WHY DO WE FEEL DISTANT EVEN THOUGH WE ARE FINALLY TOGETHER?

The Challenge
Some couples expect to feel instantly close again, but instead, they experience emotional numbness, awkwardness, or a sense of distance. This is normal! After a long separation, both partners may have adjusted to independence and need time to emotionally re-sync.

Signs of Emotional Withdrawal

- You feel disconnected, even though you miss each other deeply.
- Conversations feel surface-level rather than intimate.
- One or both spouses avoid deep emotional conversations.
- Minor irritations seem bigger than they are.

How to Overcome It

a. Acknowledge that emotional distance is a natural part of the reunification process. It doesn't mean love is lost; you're both adjusting to the new reality.

b. Ease back into closeness with small, consistent gestures (holding hands, checking in emotionally, sharing stories about time apart).

c. Try a "Daily 10-Minute Emotional Connection" exercise or spend at least 10 minutes each evening sharing at least one high and one low from the day.

d. - Ask open-ended questions: *"What's been on your mind today?" "What's something I don't know about your week?"*

e. Be patient with the process. Emotional closeness may take days or weeks to fully restore, and that's okay.

Pro Tip

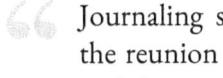 Journaling separately about your emotions after the reunion can help you identify what's missing and share it more clearly with your spouse.

2. PHYSICAL INTIMACY HESITATION: WHY DON'T WE FEEL AS PHYSICALLY CONNECTED?

The Challenge: Physical intimacy might not feel as natural or passionate as expected after a long separation. One partner may desire instant closeness, while the other may feel hesitant or uncomfortable about it.

Signs of Physical Intimacy Struggles

- One spouse is ready for sex immediately, while the other needs time.
- Physical touch (hugs, kisses, hand-holding) feels awkward or forced.
- Either partner avoids physical closeness, even though they want to reconnect.
- Past emotional wounds or stress from separation impact desire.

How to Overcome It

a. Take small, pressure-free steps toward physical closeness. Begin with gentle affection, such as holding hands, sitting close together, and offering casual touches.

b. Talk openly about physical intimacy concerns without blame. Use "I" statements:

- *"I love being close to you, but I feel like I need some time to adjust."*
- *"I missed your touch, but I also feel slightly nervous about jumping back in."*

c. Try non-sexual intimacy exercises to rebuild comfort:

- Give each other a back massage without expectations.
- Have a 3-5-minute hug challenge—hold each other in silence to rebuild comfort.
- Set a 'No Pressure' intimacy week where physical affection happens naturally but without expectation for sex.

d. If emotional wounds are present, work on emotional intimacy first. Emotional reconnection often leads to a more fulfilling physical connection.

Pro Tip

 If either spouse feels pressured, intimacy can feel forced rather than joyful. Taking it slow creates a more authentic reconnection.

3. MISMATCHED EXPECTATIONS: "WE ARE NOT ON THE SAME PAGE ABOUT RECONNECTING"

The Challenge
One partner may expect instant emotional or physical closeness, while the other needs time to adjust. This imbalance can create frustration, rejection, or misunderstandings.

Signs of Mismatched Expectations:

- One spouse is excited and ready to dive back into life together, while the other is overwhelmed by the transition.
- Differences in desires for quality time, intimacy, or personal space cause tension.
- Arguments start over minor things—not because of real conflict, but because stress levels are high.

How to Overcome It

a. Have a 'Reunion Expectations Reset' conversation. Sit down and discuss:

- *"What do you need from me in this transition?"*
- *"How can we balance closeness and personal adjustment time?"*
- *"What's something small we can do daily to reconnect?"*

b. Validate each other's experiences. Instead of saying, *"Why are you acting distant?"* try, *"I know this transition is big for both of us—what can we do to make it smoother?"*

c. Compromise by balancing closeness with space. Schedule minor, intentional connection points each day if one partner needs more time to engage.

d. If tensions rise, take a 10-minute pause. Stepping back helps regulate emotions before reacting in frustration.

<u>Pro Tip</u>

 Creating a reunion plan together—even if simple —can help set clear expectations and reduce misunderstandings.

4. EMOTIONAL BAGGAGE FROM TIME APART

During their time apart, couples experienced personal growth and meaningful change.

The Challenge

Time apart can bring about growth, stress, or personal changes that impact the relationship. If one spouse has changed their habits, mindset, or priorities, the other may struggle to adjust.

Signs That Time Apart Changed the Dynamic:

a. One or both partners may exhibit differences in their communication style, habits, or routines.
b. Past challenges from the separation resurface in minor disagreements.
c. A spouse feels "unseen" or misunderstood because of personal growth during the separation.

How to Overcome It

1. Acknowledge that change is a natural part of life, and relationships must evolve to remain strong and healthy.
2. Ask intentional questions to rediscover each other:

- *"What's something new you've learned about yourself?"*
- *"What part of your daily routine do you love now?"*
- *"How do you see our relationship evolving in this new season?"*

3. Instead of resisting change, embrace it together. Discuss how to support each other's growth while strengthening the marriage.
4. Create new shared experiences to bridge any gaps. This could be a new date night routine, a weekend activity, or a travel plan to create fresh memories.

<u>Pro Tip</u>

 Instead of expecting things to be exactly as before, celebrate the 'new version' of your marriage. Growth can bring more depth, maturity, and intimacy if embraced together.

FINAL ENCOURAGEMENT: HEALING AND RECONNECTION TAKE TIME

Rebuilding intimacy after separation isn't about 'going back'—it's about creating a stronger, deeper connection moving forward. Some days will feel easy; others may feel challenging. The key is to keep choosing each other, one intentional step at a time.

Remind Yourself

- Love doesn't disappear during separation; it needs nurturing upon return.
- Healing doesn't have a timeline. Some adjustments take days, while others take weeks or months. That's okay.
- You're not alone in this journey. Seeking support—through counseling, mentors, or trusted friends—can help navigate the transition smoothly.

MOVING FORWARD WITH LOVE AND PATIENCE

Restoring intimacy after hurt is a gradual and grace-filled process. By prioritizing emotional connection, taking small steps toward physical closeness, and seeking God's guidance, couples can rebuild trust and create a stronger, more fulfilling marriage.

Final Thought

> Above all, love each other deeply, because love covers a multitude of sins. *(1 Peter 4:8)*

CHAPTER 13

MAINTAINING INTIMACY AND PROTECTING YOUR UNION

Many couples assume that it will remain strong without additional effort once intimacy is restored. However, intimacy is not self-sustaining; it must be nurtured, protected, and consistently prioritized. Just like maintaining good health requires exercise and proper nutrition, maintaining intimacy requires intentional habits that foster emotional, physical, and spiritual closeness.

Without continuous investment, even the strongest marriages can experience emotional drift, where couples slowly disconnect without realizing it. Small moments of neglect, external pressures, and unresolved issues can create distance over time. Studies show that couples who actively maintain their intimacy report higher levels of marital satisfaction, lower stress, and stronger resilience against relational challenges (Gottman & Silver, 2021). A marriage built on consistent love and intentional connection will stand the test of time.

Intimacy Maintenance Matters

i. **Prevents Emotional Distance** – Without regular connections, couples may grow apart emotionally, making it harder to share feelings, dreams, and struggles.

ii. **Reduces the Risk of Resentment** – Neglecting intimacy allows minor irritations to escalate into deep frustrations, resulting in unresolved tension.

iii. **Strengthens Conflict Resolution** – Couples with intense intimacy are better equipped to handle disagreements with love and understanding.

iv. **Increases Relationship Security** – Feeling emotionally and physically connected helps both partners feel valued, desired, and secure.

v. **Protects Against Temptation** – A fulfilling, intimate marriage reduces the likelihood of seeking emotional or physical fulfillment outside the relationship.

Biblical Insight

 Let all that you do be done in love. – 1 Corinthians 16:14

PRACTICAL STRATEGIES TO KEEP THE CONNECTION STRONG

Maintaining intimacy doesn't require grand gestures—it's about small, daily habits that reinforce love, respect, and closeness.

1. Prioritize Daily Emotional Check-Ins

• Set aside 10–15 minutes daily to check in emotionally with your spouse.

• Ask meaningful questions:

- *How was your day, emotionally, not just logistically?*
- *Is there anything on your mind that I can support you with?*
- *What's one thing that made you smile today?*

Pro Tip

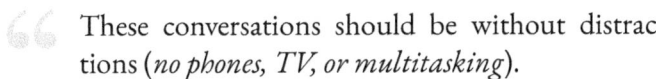 These conversations should be without distractions (*no phones, TV, or multitasking*).

2. Keep the Romance Alive with Weekly Date Nights

- Schedule a weekly or bi-weekly date night, even if it's simple (e.g., a home-cooked dinner, a nature walk, or a movie night).
- Rotate who plans the date to keep things exciting and thoughtful.
- Surprise each other with small romantic gestures (love notes, unexpected hugs, compliments).

3. Maintain Physical Affection Daily

- Increase non-sexual touch (*such as holding hands, back rubs, and morning kisses*).
- Cuddle intentionally—even just 5 minutes of close contact can boost emotional security.
- Keep sexual intimacy a priority, not an afterthought.

4. Cultivate Shared Spiritual Intimacy

- Pray together daily, even if it's just for a few minutes.

- Read Scripture as a couple and discuss how it applies to your relationship.
- Serve together—volunteering or engaging in ministry as a couple strengthens unity.

5. Keep Communicating About Your Needs

- Don't assume your spouse knows what you need— express your desires and expectations openly.
- Check in regularly with "How are we doing as a couple?"
- Practice active listening—reflect what your spouse shares before responding.

PROTECTING YOUR MARRIAGE FROM EXTERNAL THREATS

Marriage requires protection, just like any valuable relationship. Many external factors can slowly erode intimacy if not appropriately managed.

1. Work-Life Balance

Threat: Long hours, stress, and exhaustion can lead to emotional neglect.
Solution: Set clear work-life boundaries—avoid bringing work stress into your home. Make reconnection time a priority after work (*e.g., 20 minutes of uninterrupted time together before engaging in chores or responsibilities*).

2. Extended Family & Friendships

Threat: Over-involvement from family members or friends can interfere with marital unity.

Solution: Prioritize your spouse first. Set boundaries when necessary and ensure major decisions are made together.

3. Social Media & Digital Distractions

Threat: Constant screen time can replace real connection.
Solution: Create tech-free zones or times (*e.g., no phones during dinner, in the bedroom, or during conversations*).

Pro Tip

 If social media is a source of tension, agree on healthy social media boundaries to avoid conflicts related to excessive online engagement.

ADDRESSING COMMON THREATS TO INTIMACY

- **Neglect & Taking Each Other for Granted**: Over time, spouses may unintentionally stop showing appreciation or effort.
- **Solution:** Express daily gratitude for the little things. Say *"Thank you" and "I appreciate you"* often.
- **Busyness & Overcommitment**: Between work, parenting, and obligations, couples often feel too exhausted to connect.
- **Solution:** Schedule intentional time together as you would for essential tasks.
- **Unmet Expectations & Miscommunication**: Frustration builds when spouses expect unspoken needs to be met.

- **Solution:** Communicate expectations regarding chores, intimacy, finances, or emotional support.

Biblical Wisdom

> Be completely humble and gentle; be patient, bearing with one another in love. –
> *Ephesians 4:2*

ACTIVITY: THE 30-DAY MARRIAGE RECONNECTION CHALLENGE

Goal: Over the next 30 days, commit to one small act of love daily to maintain and strengthen intimacy.

Discussion Questions to Complement the 30-Day Marriage Reconnection Challenge

These questions deepen your connection as you go through the challenge. Set aside 10-15 minutes each week to discuss one or two questions, or after specific activities have been completed.

WEEK 1: EMOTIONAL CONNECTION

Theme: Rediscovering the Heart of Your Marriage.
Proverbs 5:18 – *"Let your fountain be blessed, and rejoice in the wife of your youth."*
Reflection: This verse reminds couples to celebrate their love and cherish one another. Love, joy, and romance should be cultivated intentionally, even after years of marriage.

Guiding Questions

- How can we "rejoice" in each other more intentionally?
- What are three things we cherish most about our marriage today?

Day 1 – Love Letter Reflection

- How did it feel to write a love letter to your spouse?
- What emotions or memories surfaced as you read their letter?

Day 3 – Revisiting a Favorite Memory

- What makes that memory special to you?
- What qualities about your spouse stood out to you in that moment?

Day 5 – Words of Affirmation

- What are three things you sincerely appreciate about your spouse that you haven't expressed often?
- How can we make affirming words a regular habit in our marriage?

WEEK 2: PHYSICAL & ROMANTIC RECONNECTION

Theme: The Power of Affection & Quality Time
1 Corinthians 7:3-5 – "The husband should give to his wife her conjugal rights, and likewise the wife to her husband... Do not deprive one another, except perhaps by agreement for a

limited time, that you may devote yourselves to prayer; but then come together again."

Reflection: Physical intimacy is a gift from God in marriage. It fosters unity and strengthens emotional bonds. Spouses should make a conscious effort to nurture a physical connection.

Guiding Questions:

- What are some simple ways we can express affection daily?
- How can we better communicate our needs regarding physical intimacy?

Day 8 – Unexpected Physical Affection:

- How did you feel when your spouse surprised you with affection today?
- In what ways do physical gestures (hugs, kisses, holding hands) make you feel closer emotionally?

Day 10 – No-Phone Dinner Date:

- How did removing distractions change the way we connected today?
- What are some ways we can prioritize more undistracted quality time?

Day 12 – Love Languages Check-In:

- What actions make you feel most loved and valued?
- Do you think your love language has changed over time? How can we better meet each other's needs?

WEEK 3: SPIRITUAL & MENTAL INTIMACY

Theme: Strengthening Your Marriage Spiritually &
Emotionally
Ecclesiastes 4:12 – *"Though one may be overpowered, two can
defend themselves. A cord of three strands is not quickly broken."*
Reflection: Marriage is strongest when it is centered on God.
A couple that prays together, supports one another, and
commits to mutual spiritual growth will be better equipped to
face and overcome challenges.

Guiding Questions:

- How can we invite God more into our marriage?
- What are three things we can pray for as a couple?

Day 15 – Praying Together:

- How did it feel to pray together today?
- What are some things we can consistently pray for
  as a couple?

Day 17 – Encouragement-Only Day:

- How did it feel to focus only on encouragement
  today?
- How can we reduce negativity and increase support
  in our daily conversations?

Day 19 – Managing Stress & Conflict:

- How do we typically handle stress as a couple?
- What healthier ways can we respond to each other during challenging times?

WEEK 4: CELEBRATING LOVE & GROWTH

Theme: Gratitude, Commitment, and Looking Ahead
Colossians 3:14 – *"And over all these virtues put on love, which binds them all together in perfect unity."*
Reflection: Love is the binding force in marriage. It requires daily renewal, intentional acts of kindness, and selfless commitment.

Guiding Questions:

- How can we continue prioritizing love and intimacy in our daily lives?
- What are some ways we can celebrate God's work in our marriage?

Day 22 – Looking Back at Our Journey:

- How has our relationship grown over the years?
- What are some of the biggest challenges we have overcome together?

Day 24 – Planning a Future Goal Together:

- What is one shared dream or goal that excites us?
- How can we work as a team to achieve it?

Day 28 – Small Gestures, Big Impact:

- What small things can we do daily to make each other feel loved?
- How can we keep romance alive even in busy or stressful seasons?

FINAL REFLECTION: RENEWING YOUR MARRIAGE COVENANT

Ephesians 4:2-3 – *"Be completely humble and gentle; be patient, bearing with one another in love. Make every effort to keep the unity of the Spirit through the bond of peace."*
Reflection: A lasting marriage is built on humility, patience, and effort. Marriage is a sacred covenant; maintaining intimacy requires continuous investment and selfless love.

Guiding Questions:

- What has been the biggest takeaway from this challenge?
- How can we ensure that intimacy remains a priority in every season of marriage?

Day 30 – Celebrating Our Growth:

- What did we learn about each other during this 30-day challenge?
- How has this experience strengthened our connection?
- What habits or changes do we want to carry into our daily lives?

OPTIONAL JOURNALING ACTIVITY:

Each spouse can write a short reflection at the end of the 30 days, answering:

- What was the most meaningful part of the challenge for me?
- How has my perspective on intimacy and connection changed?
- What is one commitment I want to make to strengthen our marriage moving forward?

FINAL ENCOURAGEMENT: PROTECT YOUR MARRIAGE DAILY

Remember

 Love isn't just a feeling—it's a choice and a daily investment.

- Nurture your connection every single day.
- Be proactive in protecting your intimacy from external pressures.
- Seek God's wisdom in keeping your marriage strong and fulfilling.

 When you prioritize intimacy in your marriage, you not only strengthen your emotional connection but also create a foundation of trust and understanding. This commitment to closeness helps safeguard your marriage against challenges and misunderstandings, ultimately fostering a loving and supportive partnership. Over time, this dedication to intimacy can build a lasting legacy of love that endures through life's ups and downs.

FORGIVENESS AND REBUILDING TRUST IN MARRIAGE

THE KEY TO HEALING AND RENEWAL

E very marriage faces the good, bad, and ugly moments. The bad and ugly times may bring hurt, disappointment, shame, and betrayal. These situations can result from misunderstandings, mistrust, unmet expectations, broken promises, or deeper wounds like infidelity or deception. While these experiences can shake a relationship's foundation, they do not have to define its future. The key to healing and renewal lies in forgiveness and rebuilding trust. This chapter discusses the importance of forgiveness, common obstacles to forgiving, steps for rebuilding trust, and biblical principles that guide the healing process.

Forgiveness is not just about letting go of past hurts; it is about releasing resentment and working toward genuine healing. Similarly, rebuilding trust is an intentional process that requires consistent actions, open communication, and a commitment to restoring emotional security. The Apostle Paul reminds us in *Colossians 3:13* that forgiveness is both a command and a pathway to freedom:

Bear with each other and forgive one another if any of you has a grievance against someone. Forgive as the Lord forgave you.

UNDERSTANDING FORGIVENESS IN MARRIAGE

Forgiveness in marriage is often misunderstood. Some believe it means excusing hurtful behavior or pretending as if nothing happened. However, true forgiveness is a deliberate decision to release the burden of resentment while still holding the offending spouse accountable for their actions. It is an act of grace that promotes healing for both the forgiver and the forgiven.

Forgiveness is first and foremost for the person extending it. Holding onto bitterness, anger, or resentment harms the individual more than it does the offender. Studies show that unforgiveness leads to higher levels of stress, anxiety, and even physical ailments such as high blood pressure and heart disease (*Toussaint et al., 2021*). When we forgive, we free ourselves from the emotional and spiritual burden of carrying past wounds. This is why Jesus emphasized forgiveness, not merely as a favor to others but as a means of maintaining spiritual, emotional, and physical well-being (*Matthew 6:14-15*).

Forgiveness does not mean condoning wrongdoing or instantly restoring trust; it means accepting the past and moving forward with a renewed sense of purpose. Instead, it acknowledges the reality of pain while releasing resentment and pursuing a path toward healing. This shift in perspective allows individuals to reclaim emotional freedom and prevent past wounds from dictating their future interactions and relationships.

Forgiveness in marriage is often misunderstood. Some

people believe it means excusing hurtful behavior or acting as if nothing happened. However, true forgiveness is a conscious choice to let go of resentment while still holding the offending spouse responsible for their actions. It is an act of grace that fosters healing for both the forgiver and the forgiven.

KEY REASONS FOR FORGIVENESS

Forgiveness is not just about fixing a relationship but also about personal freedom and spiritual growth. Choosing to forgive benefits the person who grants forgiveness even more than the one who receives it. It is a deliberate decision to release past wounds and start healing. Holding onto unforgiveness keeps people mentally, emotionally, and spiritually stuck in their pain, making it hard to move forward healthily. The power of forgiveness can lead to a significant improvement in one's well-being and in how relationships function (McCullough et al., 2020). Here are the main reasons why forgiveness matters:

- **Restores emotional intimacy** – Unresolved hurt creates emotional distance. Forgiveness allows couples to reconnect and grow closer.
- **Forgiveness plays a crucial role in breaking the cycle of bitterness** – Holding onto resentment only fuels further conflict, preventing true reconciliation. By choosing to forgive, individuals can disrupt this destructive cycle and pave the way for healing and restoration (*Ephesians 4:31-32*).
- **Reflects Christ's love** – Just as God forgives us, we are called to extend grace to our spouse (*Matthew 6:14-15*).
- **Promotes personal peace and mental clarity** – Forgiveness reduces mental clutter, stress, and

anxiety, leading to a healthier state of mind and heart (*Toussaint et al., 2021*).

- **Improves physical health** – Studies have demonstrated that forgiveness decreases stress, lowers the risk of cardiovascular disease, and boosts immune function (Worthington & Scherer, 2018).

- **Strengthens spiritual maturity** – Practicing forgiveness encourages spiritual discipline, humility, and a closer relationship with God. True forgiveness shows divine grace and the transformative power of love (Colossians 3:13).

- **Promotes freedom** – The choice to forgive is not about whether the offender deserves it, but about choosing freedom over bondage, peace over resentment, and healing over emotional suffering.

- **Restores emotional intimacy** – Unresolved hurt creates emotional distance. Forgiveness allows couples to reconnect and grow closer.

- **Breaks the cycle of bitterness** – Holding onto resentment only fuels further conflict, preventing true reconciliation (*Ephesians 4:31-32*).

- **Reflects Christ's love** – Just as God forgives us, we are called to extend grace to our spouse (*Matthew 6:14-15*).

- **Enhances mental and physical health** – Studies have shown that forgiveness lowers stress, reduces anxiety, and improves overall well-being (Toussaint et al., 2021).

COMMON BARRIERS TO FORGIVENESS

Despite understanding the importance of forgiveness, many individuals struggle to extend grace to others. It is crucial to identify and address the factors that hinder the forgiveness process. By understanding and overcoming these obstacles, individuals can navigate the forgiveness process more effectively.

1. Fear of Being Hurt Again
One of the biggest hurdles in forgiveness is the worry that showing grace will leave someone open to more harm. It is natural to want to protect yourself from further pain, but forgiveness doesn't mean letting yourself be mistreated. It means choosing to let go of resentment while setting healthy limits.

2. Unresolved Pain and Emotional Wounds
Forgiveness becomes difficult when past hurts are not fully processed and addressed. When pain lingers, every reminder of the offense reopens emotional wounds, making forgiveness feel impossible. Healing must be intentional and often requires time, reflection, and support.

3. Lack of Genuine Remorse from the Offender
When the person who caused the pain does not take responsibility or show remorse, forgiving can feel unjust. However, forgiveness is not about excusing their behavior but about releasing oneself from the burden of bitterness. A person can forgive without restoring complete trust immediately (*McNulty, 2019*).

4. The Desire to Claim "Right"
Many people struggle with forgiveness because they believe they have the right to hold onto their pain. They see unforgiveness as a form of justice, believing that withholding grace punishes the offender. However, the truth is that unforgiveness punishes the one holding onto it far more. Scripture teaches that God is the ultimate judge (*Romans 12:19*), and our role is to extend grace as we have received it.

5. Misconceptions About Forgiveness

Some people believe forgiving means forgetting the offense or acting as if nothing happened. Others may think forgiving requires immediate reconciliation. Neither is true. Forgiveness is a personal decision, while reconciliation requires both parties to rebuild trust over time.

6. Spiritual Maturity and Pride

Forgiveness often requires spiritual growth and a humble attitude. Those who are spiritually immature or prideful may struggle with extending grace because they see it as a sign of weakness or surrender. In contrast, Scripture teaches that forgiveness signifies strength and obedience to God (*Matthew 18:21-22*). The closer we draw to God, the easier it becomes to forgive, as we recognize the immense grace we have received. Overcoming these barriers requires a shift in perspective, an open heart to God's grace, and a willingness to prioritize healing over hurt. True forgiveness is a transformative journey that can transform marriages and the individuals involved in them.

STEPS TO PRACTICING FORGIVENESS

Forgiveness is a process, not a single event—a journey that develops gradually. Although it may not happen right away, understanding its importance and identifying the obstacles that prevent it can make the process more focused and effective. Here are practical steps that can help couples move toward true forgiveness and emotional healing.

1. Acknowledge the Hurt Honestly

Ignoring or suppressing pain does not lead to true healing. To forgive effectively, it is essential to fully recognize the emotional impact of the offense. Denial only prolongs pain; true healing begins with acknowledging, "Yes, this hurt me deeply." Without this step, resentment remains beneath the surface, making it hard to move on.

2. Process Your Emotions Before Forgiving

Forgiveness does not mean rushing past feelings of anger, sadness, or betrayal; it involves recognizing and working through them. It takes a moment to reflect on these emotions and understand their underlying causes. Prayer, journaling, or seeking wise counsel can help process the pain before truly practicing forgiveness.

3. Communicate Feelings Honestly and Respectfully

Once you've processed your emotions, it is vital to engage in open and sincere conversations with your spouse. Expressing your feelings clearly and without blame fosters understanding and helps prevent unnecessary conflicts. Instead of saying, "You never care about my feelings," consider saying, "When you did this, I felt hurt and unimportant." This approach promotes empathy and connection rather than defensiveness.

4. Separate the Person from the Action

One of the primary barriers to genuine forgiveness is perceiving a person solely through their mistakes. Clinging to an offense can cause you to see your spouse only by their wrongdoings, which hinders reconciliation. Instead, remember that a person's identity is not solely defined by their actions. Although the offense was wrong, everyone has the capacity to change and find redemption, fostering a path toward healing and growth.

5. Choose to Forgive – A Conscious Decision

Forgiveness is not just an emotional response but a deliberate choice. Even if emotions do not align immediately, forgiving initiates the healing process. Scripture reminds us that forgiveness is a command, not a suggestion(*Matthew 6:14-15*). Letting go of bitterness and embracing healing is a choice, trusting that God will bring restoration in due time.

6. Seek God's Strength and Guidance

True forgiveness often feels impossible without divine help. When hurt runs deep, asking God for strength through prayer, fasting, and scripture meditation can provide the grace needed to extend forgiveness. *Philippians 4:6-7* reminds us that through prayer, God grants peace that surpasses all understanding—even in situations where forgiveness seems unattainable.

7. Set Healthy Boundaries for Future Protection

Forgiveness does not mean allowing the same harm to happen again. Boundaries protect your emotional, mental, and spiritual health. If the offense was serious, like repeated dishonesty or betrayal, it is paramount to set clear expectations for accountability, transparency, and changed behavior to rebuild trust. Boundaries are not punishments; they are tools that foster growth and strengthen relationships.

8. Commit to Letting Go and Moving Forward

Once forgiveness is extended, it is crucial to actively release the offense instead of dwelling on it or using it as a tool for retaliation in future conflicts. This does not mean forgetting, but it means choosing not to revisit the pain over and over. Isaiah 43:18 reminds us, "Forget the former things; do not dwell on the past." Moving forward involves replacing resentment with grace, doubt with hope, and pain with healing.

9. Allow Time for Healing and Restoration

Forgiveness is a process, not a single act. Trust may take time to rebuild, and emotions may take time to align with the decision to forgive. Give yourself and your spouse grace in the journey. As *Colossians 3:13* says, *"Forgive as the Lord forgave you."* Healing is a shared effort that requires patience, consistency, and love.

10. Encourage Reconciliation but Recognize Its Limits

While forgiveness is often required, reconciliation is not always immediate or even possible. Wisdom must be exercised if the offending spouse is unrepentant, unwilling to change, or if reconciliation would lead to further harm. In such situations, forgiving for personal peace and setting boundaries that promote emotional and spiritual safety are essential. By following these steps and embracing forgiveness as a process, couples can move toward healing, renewed intimacy, and lasting peace in their marriage. Forgiveness is not just about fixing a relationship—it is about freeing yourself from the chains of past wounds and allowing God's grace to transform your heart and your marriage.

(*Source: Enright & Fitzgibbons, 2020, "Forgiveness Therapy: An Empirical Guide for Resolving Anger and Restoring Hope"*)

REBUILDING TRUST AFTER BETRAYAL

Trust is one of the most delicate aspects of marriage. It is easily broken but hard to repair. Restoring trust takes time, effort, and consistent acts of change, whether due to deception, infidelity, financial dishonesty, or emotional neglect. Trust forms the foundation of emotional security, intimacy, and marital stability (Gottman & Silver, 2022).

> Betrayal causes emotional wounds that can lead to fear, anxiety, and insecurity in the betrayed spouse. Without intentional healing, these wounds might result in ongoing suspicion, resentment, and emotional withdrawal.

However, when spouses commit to genuine repentance,

transparency, and rebuilding emotional safety, trust can be restored. Restoring trust is not just about saying, "I'm sorry." It involves demonstrating, through consistent and trustworthy actions, that the offender is committed to change (McNulty, 2019). It requires actions that match words over time. Scripture reminds us of the importance of trust in relationships. Proverbs 3:3-4 states, "Let love and faithfulness never leave you; bind them around your neck, write them on the tablet of your heart. Then you will win favor and a good name in the sight of God and man."

Love and faithfulness are essential in regaining lost trust and must be shown consistently. Rebuilding trust requires patience from both spouses. The wounded spouse must allow space to heal and undergo gradual restoration, while the offending spouse must show accountability and reliability, avoiding rushing the process. As Psalm 147:3 reminds us, "He heals the brokenhearted and binds up their wounds." Healing is a journey, not an instant event.

PRACTICAL STRATEGIES FOR REBUILDING TRUST

Rebuilding trust requires consistent effort, humility, and intentional change. Here are practical ways to restore trust in marriage after betrayal:

1. Take Full Responsibility and Acknowledge the Hurt
The offending spouse must fully accept their actions without making excuses, shifting blame, or downplaying the effect of the betrayal. Genuine remorse involves recognizing the harm caused and being open to making amends (Enright & Fitzgibbons, 2020).

2. Commit to Complete Transparency
Trust cannot be rebuilt without openness and honesty. The

offending spouse must be willing to disclose necessary information, answer complex questions, and remain accountable for their actions. If secrecy or defensiveness continues, healing is hindered. *Proverbs 11:3* states, "The integrity of the upright guides them, but their duplicity destroys the unfaithful." Integrity and transparency are essential for rebuilding trust.

3. Establish Clear Boundaries

Boundaries help protect the relationship from future breaches of trust. This could mean accountability in finances, social interactions, or digital communication. Boundaries are not about punishment, but about ensuring that both spouses feel emotionally and relationally safe. *Proverbs 4:23* warns, "Above all else, guard your heart, for everything you do flows from it." Healthy boundaries safeguard the relationship.

4. Rebuild Emotional and Physical Intimacy Gradually

Trust restoration is not just about words but about re-establishing emotional security. Simple actions such as spending quality time together, actively listening, and affirming each other help rebuild closeness. Physical intimacy may take time to restore, but emotional safety should come first (*Johnson & Zuccarini, 2021*).

5. Be Patient and Allow Time for Healing

Trust is not rebuilt overnight. The wounded spouse needs time to heal without feeling pressured to "just move on." The offending spouse must remain consistent, patient, and understanding throughout the healing process. *Ecclesiastes 3:1* reminds us, "There is a time for everything, and a season for every activity under the heavens." Healing follows its timeline.

6. Seek God and Wise Counsel

Christian couples should seek God's wisdom and guidance in the healing process through prayer, fasting, and wise counsel from trusted mentors or counselors. Healing from betrayal often requires external support (*Toussaint et al., 2021*).

7. Demonstrate Trustworthiness Through Actions

Rebuilding trust requires daily acts of integrity, honesty, and faithfulness. Actions speak louder than words, and small, consistent behaviors over time prove sincerity. As *Luke 16:10* states, "Whoever can be trusted with very little can also be trusted with much."

 Trust is not given freely after betrayal—it is earned through consistent effort and humility.

BIBLICAL PERSPECTIVE ON FORGIVENESS AND TRUST

The Bible offers timeless wisdom on forgiveness and restoring trust in relationships. While forgiveness is commanded, trust must be earned over time.

1. Forgiveness Is a Divine Mandate

- *Matthew 6:14-15* – "For if you forgive other people when they sin against you, your heavenly Father will also forgive you, but your Father will not forgive your sins if you do not forgive others."
- *Colossians 3:13* – "Bear with each other and forgive one another if you have a grievance against someone. Forgive as the Lord forgave you."
- Forgiveness is not optional for believers. It reflects God's grace and mercy. However, forgiveness does not mean trust is immediately restored.

2. Trust Must Be Rebuilt Through Faithfulness

- *Proverbs 3:5-6* – "Trust in the Lord with all your heart and lean not on your understanding; in all your ways submit to him, and he will make your paths straight."

- *Luke 16:10* – "Whoever can be trusted with very little can also be trusted with much."
- Trust is not freely given after betrayal; it must be proven through consistent actions over time.

3. Restoration Requires Humility and Accountability

- *James 5:16* – "Therefore, confess your sins to each other and pray for each other so that you may be healed."
- *Proverbs 28:13* – "Whoever conceals their sins does not prosper, but the one who confesses and renounces them finds mercy."
- Healing after betrayal requires confession, accountability, and repentance. The offender must take responsibility for their mistakes and demonstrate a willingness to change.

4. God's Grace Can Restore What Is Broken

- *Joel 2:25* – "I will restore to you the years that the locusts have eaten."
- *Psalm 147:3* – "He heals the brokenhearted and binds up their wounds."
- God specializes in restoration. A marriage that seems broken beyond repair can be healed when both spouses seek His guidance and apply biblical wisdom.

Trust is delicate, and while rebuilding may take time, God's grace enables true healing and restoration. While forgiveness is immediate, trust must be gradually rebuilt through consistent actions and spiritual renewal.

PRACTICAL EXERCISES FOR FORGIVENESS AND REBUILDING TRUST IN MARRIAGE

1. The Forgiveness Reflection Exercise
Purpose: Helps couples process hurt, identify emotions, and intentionally step toward forgiveness.
Instructions:
a. Individually Reflect: Each spouse should take time alone to answer the following questions in a journal:

- What specific event or action hurt me?
- How did this action affect me emotionally, mentally, and spiritually?
- What fears or insecurities arose as a result of this situation?
- What barriers are preventing me from forgiving my spouse?
- What would choosing to forgive bring into my life?

b. Exchange & Listen: Each spouse shares their reflections, allowing the other to listen without interrupting or defending. The listener should only respond with acknowledgment, validation, and empathy (e.g., *"I hear you," "I understand how that made you feel"*).
c. Pray Together: End by praying for God's grace, healing, and wisdom in the journey toward forgiveness. *Colossians 3:13* should be meditated on during this process.

2. The Trust-Rebuilding Commitment Plan

Purpose: Helps couples set clear, actionable steps to restore trust in their marriage.

Instructions:

a. Define Trust-Building Actions: The offending spouse should answer:

- What actions will I take to show my commitment to restoring trust?
- How will I practice openness, transparency, and accountability?
- What daily habits will I develop to reassure my spouse?

b. Establish Safe Communication: The wounded spouse should answer:

- What specific fears or triggers do I need my spouse to be mindful of?
- What reassurance do I need to feel safe again?
- How can I express my feelings in a way that promotes healing rather than resentment?

c. Mutual Agreement: Both spouses should discuss and agree on practical steps to rebuild trust, such as:

- Regular weekly check-ins to discuss progress.
- Clear boundaries (e.g., financial transparency, social accountability, time spent together).
- Commitment to openness, honesty, and emotional availability.

d. Track Progress: Each month, revisit the trust-rebuilding plan and assess:

- What progress have we made?
- What still needs improvement?
- What new habits are helping us reconnect?

3. The Reconciliation Letter Exchange

Purpose: A powerful exercise for couples to express emotions, acknowledge pain, and affirm their desire for restoration.

Instructions:

a. **Each spouse writes a letter, including the following elements:**

- Acknowledgment of the pain (e.g., *"I know that my actions caused you to feel..."*).
- An expression of sincere remorse (if applicable) or feelings of struggle regarding the pain.
- A commitment statement outlining their plans for moving forward.
- Affirmation of love and hope for their marriage.

b. **Exchange the letters and read them silently first, then out loud to each other**

After reading, discuss:

- How did it feel to write and hear these words?
- What emotions surfaced?
- What hope do we have for the future?

4. Seal the Commitment

Conclude with a prayer or a symbolic act (e.g., tearing up a piece of paper representing past hurt, lighting a candle for renewed hope, or holding hands while verbally committing to healing).

Forgiveness and trust are the pillars of a strong, enduring marriage, yet they remain among the most challenging aspects to develop after hurt and betrayal. Forgiveness isn't about forgetting or excusing the offense but about choosing healing instead of resentment. It is a gift, primarily to yourself, freeing you from the emotional weight of bitterness and creating space for personal and relational growth. Conversely, trust is not restored immediately; it must be rebuilt over time through consistency and accountability.

> The journey toward reconciliation requires patience, humility, and a deep reliance on God's wisdom and grace.

Scripture calls us to forgive as Christ forgave us (*Colossians 3:13*) and teaches us that trust is established through faithfulness and integrity (*Luke 16:10*). True restoration happens when both partners commit to honest communication, transparency, and demonstrating change through actions rather than words alone.

Healing is not a linear process, and setbacks are common. Couples can navigate this journey with hope through prayer, wise counsel, and intentional effort. God's promise of restoration (Joel 2:25) reminds us that no relationship is beyond redemption when approached with genuine repentance and a heart open to transformation. Remember that forgiveness and trust-building are ongoing processes, not one-time decisions. Whether your marriage is healing or strengthening, commit to daily acts of love, grace, and faithfulness. When God is at the center of reconciliation, what was once broken can become whole again.

These practical steps toward healing and renewal emphasize that trust and forgiveness are built over time through intentionality, grace, and effort. With perseverance, couples can establish a new foundation of love and security. The next chapter will explore how to cultivate emotional and physical intimacy after rebuilding trust, ensuring that your marriage not only survives but thrives.

CHAPTER 15

SERVING ONE ANOTHER
THE HEART OF MARITAL SUCCESS

Marriage thrives when both spouses adopt a mindset of selflessness and service. While love provides the foundation, acts of kindness, sacrifice, and support keep a marriage strong and resilient. Many marital problems arise when one or both partners prioritize their personal needs and expectations over finding ways to serve and uplift each other. This chapter explores the importance of selflessness in marriage, highlighting how mutual service strengthens emotional bonds and aligns with the biblical principle of mutual support.

SELFLESSNESS

Selflessness is the heart of a thriving marriage. It is the conscious decision to prioritize your spouse's well-being, not out of obligation but out of love. When both partners adopt a service mindset, they create a relationship built on mutual care, respect, and unwavering commitment.

Selflessness in marriage is not about neglecting one's needs, but rather about cultivating a balance where both partners seek to serve and uplift each other. When one spouse practices self-lessness, it naturally encourages the other to reciprocate, creating a cycle of love, generosity, and deep emotional connection.

SELFLESSNESS VS. SELFISHNESS

Selflessness involves a genuine willingness to compromise, especially when it comes to personal comfort, without sacrificing one's core values. It also includes regularly expressing appreciation for your spouse and putting their happiness above your own needs. On the other hand, selfishness is characterized by prioritizing one's comfort and interests, often seeking validation and acknowledgment without giving back in return. It also entails expecting love and care from your partner without offering the same in reciprocation, which can create an imbalance in the relationship.

THE IMPACT OF SELFLESSNESS IN A MARRIAGE

1. **Promotes Emotional Security:** When spouses consistently serve one another, they create a safe space where love is nurtured and emotional needs are met, providing a comforting reassurance in the relationship.
2. **Reduces Conflict:** Many marital disagreements stem from unmet expectations. A spirit of service minimizes friction as both partners actively contribute to each other's well-being, bringing a sense of peace and relief to the relationship.
3. **Encourages Gratitude:** When a spouse serves without expecting anything in return, it fosters

gratitude and appreciation, strengthening the marital bond and making each partner feel more valued and appreciated.

4. **Deepens Intimacy:** Emotional and physical intimacy flourish when spouses feel cared for, valued, and appreciated.

HOW ACTS OF SERVICE STRENGTHEN EMOTIONAL BONDS

Marriage is more than words—it is built on action. Acts of service are powerful expressions of love, often more meaningful than grand gestures or verbal affirmations. Service in marriage is about meeting each other's needs in practical, intentional ways.

Examples of Acts of Service That Strengthen Bonds

i. Preparing your spouse's favorite meal after a long day.

ii. Taking over a household chore that they usually do without being asked.

iii. Running an errand for them to lighten their load.

iv. Encouraging them when they feel discouraged or overwhelmed.

v. Praying for them daily and reminding them of God's love.

THE FIVE LOVE LANGUAGES AND ACTS OF SERVICE

Dr. Gary Chapman's *Five Love Languages* emphasizes that some people feel most loved when their spouse performs acts of service. However, even if acts of service are not your spouse's primary love language, serving in love always strengthens a marriage.

The Biblical Principle of Serving Your Spouse
Scripture consistently teaches that love is demonstrated
through service. Jesus Himself set the most remarkable example
of selfless service, teaching that true love is expressed through
humility and sacrifice.

BIBLICAL FOUNDATIONS FOR SERVING IN MARRIAGE

1. **Philippians 2:3-4** – "Do nothing out of selfish ambition or
vain conceit. Rather, in humility value others above yourselves,
not looking to your interests but each of you to the interests of
the others."
• In marriage, selflessness fosters unity, trust, and emotional
closeness.

2. **Mark 10:45** – "For even the Son of Man did not come to be
served, but to serve, and to give his life as a ransom for many."
• Jesus exemplified service as a core principle of love. Husbands
and wives are called to serve each other in the same way.

3. **Ephesians 5:25** – "Husbands, love your wives, just as Christ
loved the church and gave himself up for her."
• True love in marriage requires self-sacrificial service, not just
words of affection.

4. **Galatians 5:13** – "Serve one another humbly in love."
• Service in marriage is not about seeking praise but about
expressing love through action.

SERVING WITHOUT EXPECTING IN RETURN

One challenge in serving your spouse is avoiding the mindset of "I'll serve if they serve me first." Biblical service is about loving unconditionally. When service is motivated by genuine love rather than expectations, it fosters a culture of gratitude and mutual care within a marriage. Another challenge can be finding the right balance between serving and enabling. It's essential to serve in a way that uplifts your spouse and the relationship, rather than perpetuating dependency or neglecting your own needs.

Reflection: *How can I serve my spouse today without expecting anything in return?*

Activity: The Weekly Acts of Service Commitment

Couples should commit to one intentional act of service each week to cultivate a habit of serving one another. This exercise helps strengthen emotional intimacy and create a lasting culture of selflessness in the marriage.

Step 1: Identify Your Spouse's Needs

- Ask your spouse: *"What is one way I can serve you this week to make you feel loved and supported?"*
- Please pay attention to areas where they might need help (e.g., stress at work, fatigue, household responsibilities).

Step 2: Plan and Execute an Act of Service

- Choose one meaningful act of service and commit to doing it without announcing it.

- Examples:
- Surprise them by doing one of their least favorite chores.
- Leave an encouraging note with a thoughtful gesture.
- Handle something they usually do (e.g., packing their lunch, organizing their work materials).

Step 3: Reflect and Discuss
At the end of the week, take a few minutes to reflect together:

- *How did this act of service impact our connection this week?*
- *Did it make you feel more loved and appreciated?*
- *How can we continue serving each other intentionally?*

By making acts of service a regular part of marriage, couples reinforce their commitment to love, sacrifice, and daily connection.

CASE STUDY: SELFLESSNESS RESTORES A STRUGGLING MARRIAGE

The Problem
Michael and Sarah had been married for ten years, but their relationship had grown distant. They both felt unseen and unappreciated. Sarah felt like Michael didn't acknowledge her daily efforts at home, while Michael felt Sarah didn't value his hard work at the office.

The Turning Point
During a marriage retreat, they were challenged to serve one

another intentionally for one month. Michael started taking over some of Sarah's nightly tasks, such as putting the kids to bed, while Sarah tried to affirm Michael's hard work and prepare his favorite meals.

The Result

By the end of the month, their relationship felt revived. Small acts of service rekindled emotional intimacy, gratitude, and a sense of partnership. They realized that love was about more than just words; it was about showing care through action.

Lesson

Serving one another softens hearts, eliminates resentment, and reignites love.

CONCLUSION: THE POWER OF SERVING IN MARRIAGE

A thriving marriage is built on love in action—serving one another with humility, joy, and gratitude. Acts of service are small investments with lasting rewards, fostering connection, trust, and a deep sense of partnership.

Final Reflection Questions

1. What is one area where I can serve my spouse more intentionally?
2. How can I cultivate a heart of service rather than seeing acts of service as a duty?
3. How has serving my spouse strengthened our emotional connection in the past?

When couples choose to live selflessly, they create a joyful, Christ-focused marriage that can overcome any challenges and grow even more loving as time goes on.

SERVING ONE ANOTHER IN LONG-DISTANCE MARRIAGES

Due to military service, work-related travel, or family commitments, long-distance marriages present unique challenges. Physical separation can create emotional distance, and spouses may feel disconnected from one another's daily struggles. However, service is still possible in a long-distance relationship; it just requires creativity, consistency, and intentional effort. Couples can cultivate selflessness and service even when apart by prioritizing each other's needs and maintaining meaningful connections.

The Long-Distance Acts of Service Challenge
This challenge helps long-distance couples strengthen their connection by committing to one thoughtful act of service each week, despite the physical separation.

Week 1: Words of Affirmation Challenge

- Write a heartfelt letter or email expressing your sincere appreciation to your spouse.
- Be specific about what you admire and value in them.
- Bonus: Record a short voice or video message to make it more personal.

Week 2: Virtual Support & Encouragement

- Offer to help with something from a distance:
- If they're overwhelmed with a task, offer them research resources or solutions.

- Help plan something for their week (e.g., scheduling an appointment, organizing a surprise delivery).
- Check in on their emotional well-being and actively listen without distractions.

Week 3: Thoughtful Gift or Surprise Delivery

- Send a small, meaningful gift:
- A book they will love.
- A care package with favorite snacks.
- A handwritten letter sent via mail.
- If possible, arrange a meal or coffee delivery to brighten their day.

Week 4: Virtual Date Night

- Plan a creative online date:
- Watch a movie together while on a video call.
- Play an online game or trivia together.
- Cook the same meal and eat together over FaceTime.
- Make time for deep, uninterrupted conversation about hopes, dreams, and plans.

Bonus Challenge: Prayer & Spiritual Support

- Set a regular time to pray together via phone or text.
- Share Bible verses or devotionals that encourage each other.
- End each day with a prayer for each other's well-being.

By committing to these small acts of service, long-distance couples maintain emotional intimacy and demonstrate that love is an active choice, not just a feeling.

REAL-LIFE CASE STUDIES: THE IMPACT OF SERVING IN MARRIAGE

Case Study 1: From Frustration to Fulfillment

The Challenge
Daniel and Rebecca had been married for eight years, but their relationship became transactional over time. They divided household tasks, but their interactions felt like routines rather than acts of love. Both felt emotionally disconnected and frustrated, but neither expressed their feelings openly.

The Turning Point
Rebecca came across the idea of serving without expecting anything in return. She intentionally served Daniel every day for a week, without mentioning it or asking for anything in return. She left encouraging notes in his work bag, prepared his coffee each morning, and made an effort to ask about his day without rushing off to the next task.

By day four, Daniel noticed. He felt appreciated and emotionally connected again. He began performing small acts of service for Rebecca without being asked—handling some of her usual chores, planning a surprise date night, and initiating meaningful conversations.

The Result
Within two weeks, their marriage felt revived. They realized that small, daily acts of love were more potent than grand gestures. Serving each other broke the cycle of frustration and replaced it with appreciation and joy.

Lesson

 Selfless service softens hearts, rebuilds emotional intimacy, and fosters a culture of love.

Case Study 2: Restoring Love in a Long-Distance Marriage

The Challenge

Megan and Chris had been married for five years, but Chris was deployed overseas for military service. The time difference, stress, and lack of physical presence made communication difficult. Megan often felt emotionally disconnected and overwhelmed with managing life at home alone. Feeling powerless from afar, Chris didn't know how to offer her support.

The Turning Point

They agreed to do one small act of service for each other every week.

• Chris wrote handwritten letters, even though they mostly texted.

• Megan started recording short video messages with words of encouragement.

• They scheduled a weekly virtual date, even if only for 15 minutes.

• They prayed together over the phone every night, even just for one minute.

The Result:

Instead of focusing on the difficulties of distance, they focused on serving each other's emotional needs. Their communication deepened, and Megan no longer felt like she was struggling alone. Chris felt a strong connection to home, despite being thousands of miles away.

<u>Lesson</u>

 Love is sustained through consistent, intentional service. By prioritizing each other's emotional well-being, couples can foster closeness even when they are apart.

Final Takeaway: The Power of Serving Your Spouse

Marriage is not about personal convenience but about selfless love in action. When spouses commit to serving each other joyfully and without expectation, they build an unbreakable foundation of trust, emotional closeness, and spiritual unity.

CHAPTER 16
FAITH STRENGTHENS MARRIAGE

F ocusing on how faith can truly transform a marriage, we see that while love is the initial thread that ties two people together, faith acts as the steady anchor that keeps their connection strong through life's inevitable ups and downs. In a world full of challenges and uncertainties, sharing a common faith can create a strong foundation, turning the relationship into a resilient and lasting partnership.

It is also worth noting that couples who base their marriage on faith often find a renewed sense of unity and strength when facing financial struggles, parenting challenges, or emotional disconnect. This shared belief acts as a guiding light, helping them navigate tough times with greater resilience, clarity, and purpose. By leaning on spiritual resources that reinforce their mutual commitment, they build a sense of reassurance and confidence, highlighting how faith plays a vital role in overcoming difficulties and fostering enduring bonds.

> A faith-centered marriage is not about perfection but about pursuing God's design for love, commitment, and respect.

It is necessary to realize that a faith-centered marriage is not about perfection but about following God's plan for love, commitment, and respect. It encourages partners to be vulnerable and communicate openly, fostering a deeper connection and understanding that goes beyond surface issues. A faith-based approach often inspires couples to serve their community together, strengthening their bond as they share common values and missions that reflect their beliefs, and nurturing a more meaningful relationship.

In this context, faith acts as a guiding light, inspiring couples to prioritize their relationship and develop essential qualities such as patience, forgiveness, and understanding, which are key for long-term success. A strong marriage rooted in faith ultimately prepares partners to face life's challenges together, celebrating both the highs and lows as they journey side by side. Through faith, couples are reminded that their love is part of a greater purpose, inspiring hope and joy that endure through life's trials. With faith as their foundation, marriages can thrive, bringing fulfillment and peace to both partners.

THE BIBLICAL FOUNDATION FOR MARRIAGE

As we have noted earlier, marriage is not simply a social or legal contract; it is a profound covenant designed by God. This sacred institution goes beyond earthly arrangements and embodies a spiritual significance that mirrors the relationship between Christ and the Church, as described in Ephesians 5:25-32. It is essential to understand that the commitment to love, serve, and remain faithful to one another transcends a mere agreement between two individuals. Instead, it is a solemn vow made before God, who witnesses and blesses this union.

KEY PRINCIPLES IN SCRIPTURE

The Bible articulates several key principles that strengthen the notion of faith within marriage:

1. Faith Views Marriage as One Flesh

The significance of marriage as a covenant is underscored in Matthew 19:6, which states, "So they are no longer two, but one flesh. Therefore, what God has joined together, let no one separate." This illustrates that a divine bond exists that should not be easily severed. The concept of 'one flesh' signifies the unity and inseparability of the couple, a union that is both physical, spiritual, and emotional.

2. Faith as a Source of Strength

Psalm 127:1 declares, "Unless the Lord builds the house, the builders labor in vain." This highlights the crucial role of faith in building a solid marital foundation. The 'house' here refers to the marriage, and the verse suggests that without God's guidance and input, the couple's efforts to build a strong relationship would be in vain. Couples are encouraged to seek God's guidance and input in their relationship, reinforcing their commitment through prayer and reliance on His wisdom.

3. Love Rooted in Christ

1 John 4:19 reminds us, "We love because He first loved us." This powerful truth indicates that the love spouses share should reflect God's unconditional love for humanity. Couples can foster a deeper, more resilient bond by grounding their love in Christ.

4. The Power of Unity

In Ecclesiastes 4:12, the scripture states, "A cord of three strands is not quickly broken." This highlights the strength of unity among the couple and God in their marriage. When partners work together and include God in their relationship, they create a robust framework to withstand life's challenges.

HOW FAITH STRENGTHENS MARITAL BONDS

When couples recognize that their marriage is more than just an earthly commitment, they open the door for God's presence to permeate their relationship. This spiritual foundation provides stability, wisdom, compassion, and resilience in times of hardship, strengthening their bond and empowering them to navigate life's trials together, knowing a higher purpose supports them. As they cultivate their spiritual connection, they can foster emotional intimacy and understanding, enriching their marital journey and deepening their love.

FAITH PROMOTES SELFLESSNESS AND SACRIFICIAL LOVE

At the heart of a thriving marriage is the ability to prioritize one's spouse over oneself. This act of selflessness is crucial for nurturing love and connection, making the partner feel valued and appreciated. However, human nature often leans towards selfishness, leading to conflict, misunderstandings, and emotional disconnection between partners.

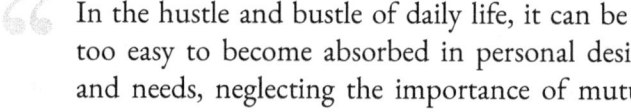

> In the hustle and bustle of daily life, it can be all too easy to become absorbed in personal desires and needs, neglecting the importance of mutual care and support.

Faith serves as a vital reminder for couples that true love transcends mere emotional gratification and is, in fact, about how they actively serve one another. This outlook encourages partners to prioritize the well-being of the other, fostering an environment of love, compassion, and mutual understanding.

 Ephesians 5:25 calls husbands to "love your wives, just as Christ loved the church and gave himself up for her."

This touching scripture highlights the depth of sacrificial love that couples are encouraged to show. Christ demonstrated this greatest love by sacrificing His life for His followers, emphasizing the importance of selflessness and dedication. Similarly, spouses who practice selfless love lay a strong foundation of trust, safety, and emotional closeness. This can be expressed through small daily acts of kindness, attentive listening, or sacrificing personal time to meet their partner's needs. When couples prioritize each other, they can build a resilient relationship that endures challenges and grows over time, resulting in a meaningful and lasting partnership.

Practical Application

- Choose daily acts of kindness that serve your spouse without expecting anything in return. These acts can be as simple as making their favorite meal, doing a household chore they dislike, or giving them a sincere compliment. Such gestures can go a long way in showing your love and care for your partner.
- Pray for a heart of humility and service in your marriage.
- Study Christ's example of sacrificial love and apply it to your relationship.

FAITH CULTIVATES FORGIVENESS AND GRACE

No marriage is immune to mistakes, misunderstandings, or even deep emotional wounds that can arise over time. These challenges are a natural part of any relationship, but resentment can accumulate if forgiveness is not practiced. This resentment becomes a barrier, creating a chasm of emotional and spiritual separation between partners. It is through the act of forgiveness that couples can begin to heal and mend these rifts.

Faith plays a significant role in the process of forgiveness. Faith teaches us that grace is not reserved solely for those who seem deserving but is a gift extended to everyone. This principle mirrors God's divine forgiveness, encouraging us to reflect this grace in our lives and relationships. Colossians 3:13 instructs us with clear guidance, "Bear with each other and forgive one another if any of you has a grievance against someone. Forgive as the Lord forgave you."

This passage reminds us that patience and forgiveness are fundamental to maintaining healthy relationships. It emphasizes the importance of understanding and compassion, urging couples to support one another in times of difficulty rather than letting grievances fester. When couples lean on God's strength and guidance, they often discover that extending grace to one another becomes more manageable. This reliance fosters reconciliation, promoting a nurturing environment where both partners feel valued and understood. By practicing forgiveness, they build a strong partnership that can weather life's unavoidable challenges. As a result, fostering a forgiving culture within a marriage deepens the connection between partners and enhances their shared spiritual growth.

Practical Application

- Establish a habit of praying together after disagreements have occurred.
- Regularly ask for and extend forgiveness with sincerity.
- Study biblical teachings on grace and apply them to marital conflicts.

FAITH STRENGTHENS RESILIENCE DURING TRIALS

Marriage is a deep journey that naturally involves various seasons of hardship. These difficulties may appear in many forms, such as illness, financial problems, significant career changes, or parenting struggles. Although faith doesn't eliminate these trials, it offers the strength and resilience needed to face them together as a couple. When facing life's challenges, James 1:2-3 reminds us that: "Consider it pure joy, my brothers and sisters, whenever you face trials of many kinds, because you know that the testing of your faith produces perseverance." This verse highlights that hardships are not just obstacles but opportunities for personal and relational growth.

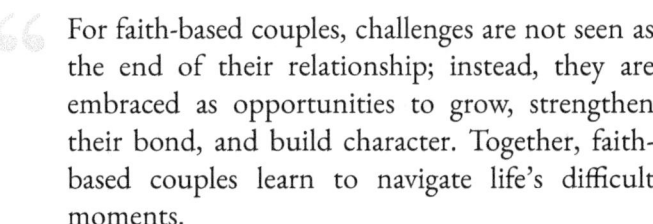

For faith-based couples, challenges are not seen as the end of their relationship; instead, they are embraced as opportunities to grow, strengthen their bond, and build character. Together, faith-based couples learn to navigate life's difficult moments.

They may face illness, for instance, as a trial that tests their commitment, but through their shared faith, they find ways to support one another emotionally and spiritually. Financial stress can spark collaboration, where open communication and shared goals are vital for overcoming obstacles. Career transitions might indicate a period of uncertainty, but faith encourages couples to trust in a plan greater than themselves. Parenting challenges also create growth opportunities, as they learn to communicate effectively and see each other's perspectives.

Ultimately, by facing these challenges together, faith-based couples endure and thrive. The trials they face are turned into opportunities that can lead to deeper intimacy, a greater understanding of each other's strengths and weaknesses, and a stronger, more resilient partnership.

Practical Application

- Lean on scripture and prayer during difficult seasons.
- Seek counsel from faith-based mentors or marriage groups.
- View hardships as a refining process rather than threats to your marriage.

FAITH CULTIVATES A STRONGER EMOTIONAL AND SPIRITUAL BOND

Many couples often encounter emotional disconnection in their relationships, which can stem from a lack of spiritual alignment. Spirituality and faith can be foundational elements that cultivate harmony among partners, influencing their core values, decision-making processes, and overall purpose in life together. When couples engage in spiritual practices such as prayer, worship, and studying scripture, they often experience increased emotional intimacy and a robust sense of satisfaction within their marriage.

Research by Wilcox and Dew (2021) supports these observations, indicating that shared spiritual practices can significantly contribute to the overall strength and fulfillment of a marital relationship. By fostering a spiritual bond, couples may navigate challenges more effectively and build a lasting connection that transcends routine interactions, leading to a more profound and enduring love.

Practical Application

- Establish a daily routine of praying together as a family.
- Read and discuss Bible passages that relate to marriage and love.
- Attend church, Bible studies, or marriage retreats to grow faith together.

BUILDING A FAITH-CENTERED MARRIAGE IN EVERYDAY LIFE

1. Prioritizing Prayer as a Couple: Prayer is one of the most potent tools for marital unity. Research indicates that couples who pray together tend to form a stronger bond and are more likely to resolve conflicts peacefully (Mahoney et al., 2021). Prayer invites God into your marriage and aligns your hearts with His will.

Practical Application

- Set aside time to pray together daily, whether in the morning, before meals, or before bed.
- Use prayer to express gratitude, seek guidance, and intercede on behalf of one another.
- Create a prayer journal where you write down

prayers for your marriage and review answered prayers.

2. Studying Scripture Together: God's Word provides wisdom and guidance for every aspect of marriage. Couples who regularly study the Bible together grow spiritually and develop a shared perspective on life's challenges.

Practical Application

- Choose a marriage-related devotional and read it together.
- Memorize key scriptures that reinforce love, unity, and perseverance.
- Discuss how biblical principles can be applied to daily marital struggles.

3. Serving God and Others Together: A faith-centered marriage extends beyond the couple's relationship—it reaches out to serve others. When couples engage in acts of service together, they not only strengthen their bond but also fulfill their spiritual purpose.

Practical Application

- Volunteer together in church ministries, outreach programs, or community service.
- Support each other's callings and ministries.
- Teach your children the value of serving God by modeling it in your marriage.

4. Faith in Long-Distance Marriages: Long-distance marriages face unique challenges, including physical separation and emotional distance, but faith provides the stability necessary to endure these periods of separation. Couples who maintain their spiritual connection while apart build resilience, trust, and a deeper understanding of each other. By engaging in shared spiritual practices, such as prayer or meditation, they create a sense of unity, despite the miles that separate them. This spiritual bond helps them cope with the loneliness that often accompanies long-distance relationships and strengthens their commitment to one another. In this way, faith becomes a cornerstone upon which these couples can rely, allowing them to navigate their challenges with hope and love.

Practical Application

- Schedule virtual prayer meetings to stay spiritually connected.
- Read devotionals or Bible passages together, even if you are in different locations.
- Seek encouragement from Christian communities that understand the challenges of long-distance marriage.

FAITH-BASED MARRIAGE CHALLENGE: 30 DAYS OF SPIRITUAL CONNECTION

To make faith a daily priority, couples can commit to the following 30-Day Spiritual Connection Challenge:

- Days 1-5: Pray together for five minutes each day.
- Days 6-10: Read and discuss a Bible passage about love and commitment.
- Days 11-15: Write a prayer for your spouse and share it.

- Days 16-20: Attend a church service or faith-based event together.
- Days 21-25: Perform an act of service together.
- Days 26-30: Reflect on how faith has strengthened your marriage and set spiritual goals for the future.

In essence, a faith-centered marriage is not only a union of two individuals but a divine partnership that nurtures growth, resilience, and profound love. When couples commit to walking this spiritual path together, whether through prayer, scripture, service, or unwavering trust, they build an unbreakable bond rooted in divine strength. Such a marriage becomes a beacon of hope and a catalyst for positive influence, radiating blessings that extend into families, communities, and generations to come. Embracing faith as the foundation ensures that love endures life's storms and flourishes in the light of divine grace.

CHAPTER 17

LEAVING A LASTING LEGACY

BUILDING A MARRIAGE THAT INSPIRES FUTURE GENERATIONS

As we have learned throughout this book, marriage is a legacy that extends far beyond the present moment. How couples love, serve, and commit to each other profoundly influences their children, family, community, and even future generations. A strong marriage becomes a testimony of faith, resilience, and love that inspires others. Yet, legacy-building does not happen by chance—it requires intentional effort, shared vision, and a deep commitment to values that will stand the test of time.

THE POWER OF MARRIAGE AS A LEGACY

Sociologists and family researchers emphasize that a strong marriage provides stability that ripples across generations. Studies show that children who grow up in homes where parents model healthy conflict resolution, mutual respect, and emotional connection are more likely to establish successful relationships (McLanahan & Beck, 2020). Conversely, when marriage is marked by instability or disconnection, children often struggle with trust, commitment, and relational security in adulthood (Amato & James, 2020).

Marriage is not just about companionship in the present; it is also about companionship in the future. It is about shaping the future. Each interaction, choice, and sacrifice within a marriage either strengthens or weakens the foundation upon which future generations will build their relationships (Wilcox & Dew, 2020).

 Every couple must ask themselves: What kind of marital legacy are we leaving behind?

1. PASSING DOWN CORE VALUES IN MARRIAGE

A marriage legacy is not simply about staying together for a lifetime—it is about the values and principles couples pass down to their children and those who look up to them. A study by Wilcox (2022) highlights that strong marriages are often founded on shared values, particularly in the areas of faith, commitment, service, and perseverance. These shared values unite couples and have the power to shape their children's worldview and relational expectations, inspiring them to build strong marriages of their own.

FAITH AND SPIRITUAL COMMITMENT

Undoubtedly, faith plays a transformative role in building a marriage legacy. Research indicates that couples who prioritize spiritual intimacy through prayer, worship, and shared biblical values tend to report higher levels of marital satisfaction and long-term stability. This emphasis on faith can provide a strong foundation for a marriage, offering reassurance and hope even in the face of challenges (Pargament, 2021).

When children witness parents seeking God together, making faith-based decisions, and using scripture as their guide in marriage, they internalize these lessons and apply them in their future relationships.

 Joshua 24:15 declares, *"As for me and my house, we will serve the Lord."* A marriage committed to faithfulness to God leaves a spiritual inheritance that extends beyond the couple.

Practical Application

- Develop family traditions centered around faith, such as praying together before meals, attending church as a family, and reading scripture as a couple.
- Share testimonies of how God has sustained your marriage through difficult seasons.

2. COMMITMENT AND PERSEVERANCE THROUGH TRIALS

A key component of a marital legacy is demonstrating resilience in the face of challenges. Marriage is not immune to difficulties, but couples who work through struggles together, rather than opting for separation, provide a model of perseverance. This resilience empowers them to overcome obstacles and teaches their children that love is a commitment, not just an emotion (Cherlin, 2021).

Case Study: Michael and Lisa faced financial struggles early in their marriage. Rather than allowing stress to pull them apart, they committed to open communication, budgeting together, and leaning on faith. Today, their grown children handle financial challenges in their marriages with the same patience and teamwork they witnessed in their parents.

Practical Application

- Commit to working through difficult seasons rather than avoiding them.
- Share stories of perseverance with your children and loved ones to normalize resilience in marriage.

3. SERVING ONE ANOTHER AS A MODEL FOR LOVE

Serving one another in marriage is a powerful way to cultivate a legacy of love and selflessness. Research by Scuka (2021) highlights that acts of service between spouses, such as caring for each other's needs, showing kindness, and prioritizing one another, enhance emotional intimacy and provide a model for future generations to emulate. This service is not just a duty, but a way to show love and appreciation for your spouse.

Jesus' servant leadership model in John 13:14-15, where He washes His disciples' feet, reminds us that true greatness comes from serving others. In marriage, this principle manifests in small, daily acts of love, such as preparing a meal for a tired spouse, offering encouragement, or providing emotional support.

Practical Application

- Practice daily acts of service for your spouse, demonstrating love in practical ways.
- Involve your children in service projects, teaching them that marriage is about giving, not just receiving.

PROTECTING AND STRENGTHENING A MARRIAGE LEGACY

A marital legacy must be actively protected from external pressures that could weaken its foundation. Modern distractions, such as demanding careers, social media, and societal pressures, can pull couples apart if not managed wisely. Research by Fowers (2019) suggests that couples who prioritize their marriage by setting boundaries and making time for each other are more likely to pass down healthy relational habits. Setting boundaries is not a sign of weakness, but a way to empower your marriage.

1. Prioritizing Time Together

One of the most common challenges in long-term marriages is the gradual drift that can occur due to busyness. Couples who intentionally schedule time for one another, whether through date nights, vacations, or shared hobbies, strengthen their bond and create lasting memories.

Practical Application

- Establish a weekly or monthly marriage check-in to discuss priorities, emotions, and relational goals.
- Create "non-negotiable" time together, free from work or digital distractions.

2. Protecting Your Marriage from Negative Influences

In today's world, negative cultural narratives often undermine the sanctity of marriage. Whether through media portrayals that normalize infidelity or social circles that encourage selfishness, couples must actively guard their relationship against harmful influences. Studies by Kenny, Kashy, and Cook (2021) emphasize that maintaining firm boundaries and surrounding oneself with positive marriage role models significantly contributes to relationship success.

Practical Application

- Be mindful of the content you consume—prioritize media that uplifts marriage rather than devalues it.
- Surround yourself with couples who encourage and support strong marriages.

LEGACY-BUILDING CHALLENGE: CREATING A MARITAL TESTAMENT

Couples can participate in the Marital Testament Challenge to make legacy building more practical and meaningful. This intentional exercise documents their shared values, lessons, and hopes for the future.

Step 1: Define Your Marriage Mission Statement
Sit together and write a short mission statement reflecting your core beliefs and values as a couple. Answer questions such as:

- What do we want our marriage to stand for?
- What biblical principles do we want to guide our relationship?
- What do we hope to pass to our children or others looking up to us?

Step 2: Write a Letter for Future Generations
Each spouse writes a letter to their children, grandchildren, or future generations, sharing wisdom about love, faith, perseverance, and what they have learned about marriage. These letters

can be stored and read years later or passed down as part of a family tradition.

Step 3: Document Key Marriage Lessons

- Create a "Marriage Legacy Journal" where you document:
- Milestones and memories that shaped your relationship.
- Stories of God's faithfulness in your marriage journey.
- Lessons learned from challenges and how they strengthened your bond.

Step 4: Establish a Tradition of Teaching and Mentorship
Couples who have built a strong marriage can extend their legacy by mentoring younger couples or newlyweds. Research by Chapman (2022) suggests that couples who engage in marriage mentorship find deeper meaning and purpose in their relationship.

Practical Application

- Start a small group or host marriage workshops at your church to support couples in your community.
- Be intentional about guiding and encouraging younger couples.

A marriage built on faith, commitment, and service benefits the couple, shapes families, influences communities, and has a lasting impact on generations to come. Legacy-building is an ongoing process that requires intentionality, wisdom, and

God's grace. Couples who prioritize their marriage as a sacred institution, model biblical love, and invest in the next generation create a lasting impact that extends far beyond their lifetime.

 As Proverbs 13:22 reminds us, *"A good man leaves an inheritance to his children's children."*

This inheritance is not just financial; it is a spiritual and relational foundation that shapes the future.

WHAT LEGACY WILL YOUR MARRIAGE LEAVE BEHIND?

Reflection Questions for Couples: At the end of this chapter, these reflection questions will help couples engage deeply with the legacy-building challenge and apply the principles in their marriage:

1. What values do we want to define in our marriage legacy?
2. How do we demonstrate love, faith, and commitment in ways that future generations can learn from?
3. What traditions or habits can we establish that reinforce our marriage legacy (e.g., prayer routines, annual marriage retreats, service projects)?
4. Who are the couples we look up to as examples of a strong marriage, and what qualities do we admire in them?
5. What challenges have we overcome that have strengthened our marriage and serve as a testimony to others?

6. How can we ensure that our children (or those we mentor) understand the importance of forgiveness, perseverance, and faith in marriage?
7. How can we serve other couples and pass on the lessons we've learned about marriage?
8. If someone were to describe our marriage in 20 years, what do we hope they would say about it?
9. What steps can we take to align our marriage more closely with the biblical principles of love, service, and unity?
10. How can we document and share our marriage journey, through letters, journals, videos, or books, so that future generations can benefit from our experiences?

FINAL WORDS &
ENCOURAGEMENT
FOR MARRIAGES THAT ENDURES

> Marriage is a lifelong journey, one filled with
> seasons of joy, challenge, growth, and renewal.

Every chapter of this book explores the essential elements that strengthen and sustain a thriving marriage: love, trust, intimacy, forgiveness, service, and legacy. While knowledge and insights are valuable, true transformation comes from application.

As you close this book, I encourage you to apply what you have learned and make it a reality. Marriage is not simply about staying together; it is about growing together, deepening your bond, and honoring the covenant you made before God and each other.

SUSTAINING WHAT YOU HAVE LEARNED

1. Make Love an Action, Not Just a Feeling
Love transcends mere emotions; it's a daily commitment to serve, uplift, and cherish one another. While feelings may

change, dedication stays strong when love is deliberately practiced.

2. Build and Maintain Intimacy

Never stop pursuing emotional, physical, and spiritual closeness. Intimacy is not automatic—it requires intentional effort. Prioritize quality time, open communication, and mutual affection to keep the connection alive.

3. Keep Christ at the Center

A marriage rooted in faith, prayer, and God's Word will stand firm against trials. Lean on God in every season, and He will sustain your union. Remember Matthew 19:6:

"So they are no longer two, but one flesh. Therefore, what God has joined together, let no one separate."

4. Forgive Often and Extend Grace

No marriage is without mistakes, disappointments, or misunderstandings. Choose forgiveness over resentment, grace over judgment, and love over pride. A healthy marriage is built on mercy, humility, and the willingness to give second chances.

5. Protect Your Marriage from Disconnection

Life's demands—work, stress, responsibilities—can pull couples apart if they are not careful. Prioritize each other amid the busyness of life. Regularly check in, affirm your love, and intentionally reconnect and nurture your relationship.

6. Leave a Lasting Legacy

We have already established that marriage is not merely a union of two individuals in the present moment; it encompasses a profound commitment that extends far beyond our current lives. It is about the love, faith, and values that we consciously cultivate together, and these elements play a crucial role in shaping the lives of future generations. By nurturing strong relationships and instilling meaningful principles, we create a lasting legacy that can positively influence our children, their children, and generations to come. Remember, your commitment today lays the groundwork for tomorrow's impact, ensuring that the bonds of love you share radiate through time, knitting together your family's future with threads of enduring affection and shared ideals.

A CALL TO ACTION: KEEP BUILDING, KEEP LOVING, KEEP GROWING

Marriage is a sacred gift that requires stewardship, care, and devotion. It is a relationship designed to mirror Christ's love—a sacrificial, unconditional, and enduring love. No matter where you are in your marriage journey—whether you are newlyweds, facing challenges, or enjoying a strong season—keep building.

- Keep loving with intention.
- Keep choosing commitment over convenience.
- Continue to lean on God for wisdom and strength.

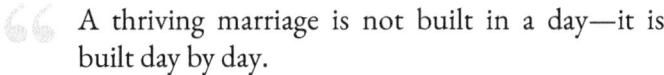 A thriving marriage is not built in a day—it is built day by day.

Prayer

May your marriage reflect God's love, a source of strength and joy, and a testimony of grace and faithfulness. May you grow deeper in love, wisdom, and unity, and may your marriage be a lasting legacy of hope and inspiration for future generations.

COUPLES RECONNECTION PLAN

A GUIDED EXERCISE FOR EMOTIONAL AND PHYSICAL RECONNECTION

GUIDED EXERCISE FOR EMOTIONAL AND PHYSICAL RECONNECTION.

Instructions

- Find a quiet, comfortable space to complete this together.
- Each spouse should answer the questions individually first, then share and discuss.
- Be open, patient, and understanding throughout the process.

STEP 1: ACKNOWLEDGE WHERE YOU ARE NOW

Before rebuilding intimacy, reflecting on your current relationship status is essential.

Individual Reflection (Write Down Your Answers):

1. How would you describe our emotional connection right now? (e.g., strong, distant, improving, strained, in transition, etc.)
2. What do you miss most about our relationship?
3. What has changed in our relationship during this time apart (or after trust was broken and restored)?
4. What are some barriers keeping us from feeling fully connected again? *(e.g., past pain, unresolved emotions, stress, communication struggles, fear of rejection, routine differences, etc.)*

Couple Discussion
Share your reflections.

- Use active listening (*nodding, eye contact, paraphrasing your spouse's words*).
- Avoid interrupting or getting defensive—this is about understanding each other's perspective.

STEP 2: IDENTIFY YOUR NEEDS, LOVE LANGUAGES, AND APOLOGY LANGUAGES

Understanding each other's emotional and physical needs, as well as knowing your partner's preferred Love and Apology Languages, creates a roadmap for more robust reconnection and practical reconciliation.

Personal Reflection

- **Emotional Connection:** What makes you feel emotionally connected to me? *(Examples: Deep conversations, shared activities, words of affirmation, quality time, acts of service, etc.)*

- **Physical Connection:** What makes you feel physically connected to me? *(Examples: Holding hands, hugs, cuddling, sexual intimacy, playfulness, etc.)*
- **Love Language:** What is your primary love language, and how would you like me to express it this week?
- **Apology Language:** What is your primary apology language? *(Expressing regret, Accepting responsibility, Making restitution, Genuinely repenting, Requesting forgiveness, Providing an explanation, or Making amends.)* How would you like me to apply this knowledge when conflicts arise?
- **Intimacy Building:** What is one specific action I could do this week to help you feel emotionally closer to me?
- **Reconnection Activity:** What is one specific activity you would like to do together to rebuild intimacy?

Couple Discussion

- Share your responses openly and listen attentively to your partner's answers.
- Discuss your primary love and apology languages, highlighting how this knowledge can help you better navigate conflicts and foster intimacy.
- Identify one immediate action each of you will take based on your partner's identified needs, love language, and apology language.

Pro Tip

If you have not already identified your spouse's love and apology languages, take The Five Love Languages Quiz and The Seven Apology Languages Quiz together. Understanding these personal preferences can significantly enhance the effectiveness of how you express love and apologies, ultimately deepening your emotional and relational connection.

STEP 3: CREATE A RECONNECTION RITUAL

Small, consistent actions are the key to rebuilding intimacy. Choose one or more rituals to do daily or weekly.

Pick at least one of these daily connection points:

- **Morning Check-In:** Spend 5 minutes in the morning sharing a goal, prayer, or affirmation for the day.
- **Evening Wind-Down:** Set aside time at night to reflect on your day, sharing highs and lows, funny moments, and lessons learned.
- **The 30-Second Hug:** Hold each other for at least 30 seconds daily to create a sense of safety and bonding.
- **Scheduled Quality Time:** Block out one hour or more weekly for undistracted time together, free from phone and work distractions.
- **Faith-Based Connection:** Pray together or read scripture related to love and commitment (*Ephesians 4:2-3, Colossians 3:14, 1 Corinthians 13:4-7*).
- **Shared Fun:** Watch a show together, play a game, or cook a meal together.

STEP 4: PLAN A MEANINGFUL RECONNECTION ACTIVITY

Choose a special activity to rekindle emotional and/or physical intimacy.

Ideas for Emotional Intimacy

- Write a love letter to each other and read it aloud.
- Take a walk together and talk about your future dreams.
- Do a "First Date Re-creation"—go to the place where you had your first date and relive the moment.

Ideas for Physical Intimacy (Non-Sexual & Sexual)

- Have a "Cuddle Challenge"—hold each other for 5 minutes every night without distractions.
- Try a Slow Dance Night—play your favorite song and dance together in your living room.
- Plan a romantic evening with candles, music, and an intentional focus on each other.

Pro Tip

For long-distance couples, schedule a virtual date where you watch the same movie, cook the same meal, or play a game together online.

STEP 5: SET RELATIONSHIP GOALS FOR THE NEXT 30 DAYS

Growth occurs when there is intentional effort. Pick 1-3 goals to focus on over the next month. These goals are not just tasks, but opportunities for growth and a stronger relationship.

Emotional Goal: *Engage in a meaningful conversation at least three times per week.*
Physical Goal: *Increase non-sexual touch (e.g., hugs, hand-holding, kisses) daily.*
Spiritual Goal: *Pray together every night before bed.*

Pro Tip

> Schedule a check-in at the end of 30 days to reflect on what has improved and what still needs work.

FINAL STEP: COMMIT TO EACH OTHER

Now that you've created a plan, it's crucial to seal your commitment with a verbal or written affirmation. This commitment is a powerful tool in strengthening your connection, understanding each other's needs, and prioritizing your relationship. No matter your challenges, choosing each other and your relationship daily is the key to success.

Say this to each other (or write it in a note)

"I commit to strengthening our connection, understanding your needs, and prioritizing our relationship. No matter what challenges we face, I choose you, and I choose us—every single day."

Keep this plan somewhere visible, such as on your fridge, in a journal, or saved on your phone, as a reminder of your commitment. This will serve as a daily reminder of your shared goals and the steps you are taking to achieve them.

FINAL ENCOURAGEMENT: HEALING TAKES TIME

Remember, reconnecting isn't about rushing back to what was —it's about building something even more profound and stronger moving forward.

- **Be patient.** Remember, restoring intimacy is a journey, not a race. It's okay if it takes time. Your patience will be rewarded with a deeper, more meaningful connection. Manage your expectations and understand that progress may not always be linear. There will be ups and downs, but your kindness and understanding will be a source of comfort and support for each other.
- **Be kind to each other.** Healing and reconnection aren't always straightforward. There will be ups and downs, but your kindness and understanding will be a source of comfort and support for each other. Remember, your partner is also on this journey, and your kindness can make a significant difference.
- **Celebrate progress.** Every small step towards intimacy is a victory. Recognizing and celebrating these moments will keep you motivated and optimistic about the journey ahead. Remember, it's not just about the destination but also the journey. Your love is worth the effort. Keep choosing each other every day.

Your love is worth the effort.
Keep choosing each other every day.

30-DAY MARRIAGE RECONNECTION CHALLENGE

The "30-Day Marriage Reconnection Challenge" aims to foster deeper connections between partners through thoughtful discussions and reflections on Scripture. This challenge, designed to enrich your marriage, includes discussion questions that encourage couples to explore their relationship and deepen their spiritual intimacy by considering relevant biblical passages.

WEEK 1: EMOTIONAL CONNECTION

Theme
Rediscovering the Heart of Your Marriage
Scripture Reflection
Proverbs 5:18 - *Let your fountain be blessed, and rejoice in the wife of your youth.*
Reflection
This verse joyfully reminds couples to celebrate their love and cherish one another. Love, joy, and romance should be cultivated intentionally, even after years of marriage, bringing the couple a sense of upliftment and inspiration.

Discussion Questions

- How can we "rejoice" in each other more intentionally?
- What are three things we cherish most about our marriage today?
- How can we create more meaningful moments together this week?

WEEK 2: PHYSICAL & ROMANTIC RECONNECTION

Theme
The Power of Affection & Quality Time
Scripture Reflection
1 Corinthians 7:3-5
The husband should give to his wife her conjugal rights, and likewise the wife to her husband... Do not deprive one another, except perhaps by agreement for a limited time, that you may devote yourselves to prayer; but then come together again.
Reflection
Physical intimacy, a gift from God in marriage, is a powerful tool that fosters unity and strengthens emotional bonds. Spouses should consciously nurture this physical connection, which can help them feel more connected and emotionally strengthened.
Discussion Questions

- What are some simple ways we can express affection daily?
- How can we better communicate our needs regarding physical intimacy?

- What romantic gestures make us feel most loved and appreciated?

WEEK 3: SPIRITUAL & MENTAL INTIMACY

Theme
Strengthening Your Marriage Spiritually & Emotionally
Scripture Reflection
Ecclesiastes 4:12
Though one may be overpowered, two can defend themselves. A cord of three strands is not quickly broken.
Reflection
Marriage is strongest when it is centered on God. A couple that prays together, supports one another, and commits to mutual spiritual growth will be better equipped to withstand challenges, providing a sense of reassurance and security to the couple.
Discussion Questions

- How can we invite God more into our marriage?
- What are three things we can pray for as a couple?
- How can we better support each other's emotional well-being?

WEEK 4: CELEBRATING LOVE & GROWTH

Theme
Gratitude, Commitment, and Looking Ahead
Scripture Reflection
Colossians 3:14
And over all these virtues put on love, which binds them all together in perfect unity.

Reflection

Love is the binding force in marriage. It requires daily renewal, intentional acts of kindness, and selfless commitment.

Discussion Questions

- How can we continue prioritizing love and intimacy in our daily lives?
- What are some ways we can celebrate God's work in our marriage?
- How can we set goals for continued growth in our marriage?

FINAL REFLECTION: RENEWING YOUR MARRIAGE COVENANT

Ephesians 4:2-3

Be completely humble and gentle; be patient, bearing with one another in love. Make every effort to keep the unity of the Spirit through the bond of peace.

Reflection

A lasting marriage is built on humility, patience, and effort. Marriage is a sacred covenant; maintaining intimacy requires continuous investment and selfless love.

Final Discussion Questions

- What has been the biggest takeaway from this challenge?
- How can we ensure intimacy remains a priority in every season of our marriage?
- What specific commitment will we make to strengthen our marriage moving forward?

May this challenge inspire a robust connection, renewed love, and a strengthened bond in your marriage.

APPENDICES & BONUS CONTENT

This section provides a convenient array of tools and resources designed to help couples apply, review, and reinforce the principles discussed in this book. Whether you need a quick reference, supplementary readings, or a structured method to evaluate your marriage regularly, these appendices are here to provide practical guidance and support for your journey.

APPENDIX A: PRACTICAL EXERCISES INDEX

(All Activities Summarized for Easy Reference)

This index is a comprehensive compilation of all the exercises, challenges, and practical applications scattered throughout the book. It's a reliable resource for quick reference, ensuring you're fully prepared to tackle any aspect of your marriage.

1. Strengthening Communication & Conflict Resolution

These exercises have the potential to transform your communication and conflict resolution skills, paving the way for a more harmonious and understanding relationship.

- The Listening Challenge – Practice active listening by setting aside 10 minutes daily to listen without interrupting or offering solutions.
- The Cooling-Off Agreement – A structured approach to de-escalating heated arguments with a time-out process.
- Conflict Resolution Reflection and Application: Utilize journaling and self-awareness worksheets to monitor emotional responses and enhance reactions to conflict.

2. Enhancing Emotional & Physical Intimacy

- The Reconnection Plan – A step-by-step guide to restoring emotional and physical closeness after a period of distance or hurt.
- The Weekly Touch Challenge – Increasing physical affection in non-sexual ways (hugging, hand-holding, cuddling, etc.).
- The Intimacy Inventory – A reflective exercise to assess emotional, physical, and spiritual intimacy levels in the marriage.

3. Financial Intimacy & Marriage Stability

- The Money Mindset Exercise – Identifying personal financial habits and discussing financial goals as a couple.
- The Debt-Free Together Plan: Strategies for working as a team to eliminate financial stress and manage household finances.

4. Forgiveness & Rebuilding Trust

- The Forgiveness Reflection Exercise – Guided journaling questions to help process emotions and take steps toward forgiveness.
- The Trust-Rebuilding Commitment Plan – A structured plan for transparency, accountability, and restoring trust after betrayal.
- The Reconciliation Letter Exchange – Writing heartfelt letters to acknowledge pain and express commitment to healing.

5. Serving & Supporting One Another

- The Weekly Acts of Service Commitment – A structured challenge encouraging spouses to serve each other intentionally every week.
- The Long-Distance Service Challenge – Creative ways to serve and stay connected for couples in long-distance marriages.

6. Marriage Legacy & Growth

- The 30-Day Marriage Reconnection Challenge – A daily guide for rekindling emotional and physical closeness.
- The Legacy-Building Challenge – Identifying values, traditions, and lessons to pass on to future generations.

APPENDIX B: SUPPLEMENTAL READINGS & RECOMMENDED RESOURCES

For further study and growth, the following books, articles, and studies provide deeper insights into marriage, relationships, and faith-based principles.

RECOMMENDED BOOKS

1. The Meaning of Marriage – Timothy Keller
2. Sacred Marriage – Gary Thomas
3. The 5 Love Languages – Gary Chapman
4. The 7 Apology Languages – Aigbefo Ehihi
5. Love & Respect – Emerson Eggerichs
6. The Seven Principles for Making Marriage Work – John Gottman
7. Boundaries in Marriage – Henry Cloud & John Townsend
8. His Needs, Her Needs – Willard Harley

FAITH-BASED MARRIAGE RESOURCES

• Focus on the Family – Marriage and family life resources (www.focusonthefamily.com)
• Desiring God – Biblical perspectives on love and relationships (www.desiringgod.org)
• FamilyLife Today – Practical biblical advice for couples (www.familylife.com)
Marriage Counseling & Support
• Gottman Institute – Research-based marriage counseling and resources (www.gottman.com)
• Prepare/Enrich – Marriage assessment and counseling tools (www.prepare-enrich.com)

APPENDIX C: MARRIAGE CHECK-UP CALENDAR TEMPLATE

The 'Marriage Check-Up Calendar' is a proactive tool that provides a structured yet flexible way for couples to schedule regular conversations about their relationships. It's designed to help you prioritize and maintain a healthy marriage.

How to Use This Calendar

- Set aside time each month for a "Marriage Check-In" conversation.
- Use guided questions to assess communication, intimacy, finances, and overall satisfaction.
- Commit to actionable steps based on insights gained from your discussions.

Month	Focus Area	Guided Questions	Action Steps
January	Communication	Are we truly listening to each other? How can we improve our conversations?	Practice active listening for 10 minutes daily.
February	Intimacy	How emotionally connected do we feel? What can we do to strengthen closeness?	Plan a weekend getaway or special date night.
March	Conflict Resolution	What unresolved issues need addressing? Are we handling disagreements well?	Use the Cooling-Off Agreement during conflicts.
April	Family & Priorities	How are we managing responsibilities? Are we balancing work, family, and marriage effectively?	Schedule intentional family bonding time.
May	Spiritual Growth	Are we praying together? How can we grow spiritually as a couple?	Start a joint Bible study or devotional.
June	Finances	Are we financially aligned? What adjustments do we need to make?	Review the budget together and set financial goals.

Month	Focus Area	Guided Questions	Action Steps
July	Love & Affection	How well are we expressing love to each other? What love language needs more attention?	Complete the Weekly Touch Challenge.
August	Serving Each Other	Are we prioritizing acts of service? What small ways can we show appreciation?	Do one intentional act of service per week.
September	Future Planning	What dreams or goals do we have for the future? How are we progressing?	Set new couple goals for the next 6 months.
October	Health & Well-Being	How are we caring for our physical and emotional health? Are we supporting each other?	Commit to a healthy habit together (exercise, diet, etc.).
November	Gratitude & Reflection	What are we most thankful for in our marriage? How can we cultivate more gratitude?	Write letters of appreciation to each other.
December	Year-End Review	What went well this year? What needs improvement? What will we commit to in the new year?	Set new intentions and goals for the next year.

This Marriage Check-Up Calendar helps couples stay connected, accountable, and proactive in maintaining a healthy marriage.

FINAL THOUGHTS

Marriage is a dynamic, ever-growing relationship that requires intention, commitment, and faith. These resources, exercises, and templates are designed to support and strengthen your marriage, whether you are newlyweds or have been together for decades.

The key to a thriving marriage is continuous invest-ment in love, effective communication, and a shared vision for the future.

As you move forward, commit to growing together, serving each other, and keeping God at the center of your relationship. May your union be blessed, fruitful, and a testimony of enduring love.

REFERENCE LIST

Chapter 2

Gottman, John & Silver, Nan. (2022). The Seven Principles for Making Marriage Work. Harmony Books.

Chapman, Gary. 1995. The 5 Love Languages: The Secret to Love That Lasts. Northfield Publishing.

Stanley, Scott. 2014. Fighting for Your Marriage. Jossey-Bass.

McNulty, J. K. (2019). The Dynamics of Marital Trust and Repair. Journal of Marriage and Family Studies, 81(4), 689-702.

Chapter 3

Eggerichs, Emerson. Love and Respect: The Love She Most Desires; The Respect He Desperately Needs. Thomas Nelson, 2004.

Gottman, John. The Seven Principles for Making Marriage Work. New York: Harmony Books, 1999.

Gottman, John & Silver, Nan. (2022). The Seven Principles for Making Marriage Work. Harmony Books.

Keller, Timothy. The Meaning of Marriage: Facing the Complexities of Commitment with the Wisdom of God. Penguin Books, 2011.

McNulty, J. K. (2019). The Dynamics of Marital Trust and Repair. Journal of Marriage and Family Studies, 81(4), 689-702.

Miles, C. A. (2006). The Redemption of Love: Rescuing Marriage and Sexuality from the Economics of a Fallen World. Brazos Press.

Miles, Carrie A. The Redemption of Love: Rescuing Marriage and Sexuality from the Economics of a Fallen World. Brazos Press, 2006.

Sollee, Diane. Smart Marriages. Accessed via SmartMarriages.com.

Stanley, S. (2014). Fighting for Your Marriage. Jossey-Bass.

Chapter 4

Johnson, Sue. Hold Me Tight: Seven Conversations for a Lifetime of Love. Little, Brown Spark, 2008.

Orbuch, Terri. 5 Simple Steps to Take Your Marriage from Good to Great. Delacorte Press, 2012.

Hendrix, Harville. Getting the Love You Want: A Guide for Couples. St. Martin's Griffin, 1988.

Chapman, Gary. The 5 Love Languages: The Secret to Love That Lasts. Northfield Publishing, 1995.

Sollee, Diane. Smart Marriages. Accessed via SmartMarriages.com.

Chapter 5

Chapman, Gary. The 5 Love Languages: The Secret to Love That Lasts. Northfield Publishing, 1995.

Hendrix, Harville. Getting the Love You Want: A Guide for Couples. St. Martin's Griffin, 1988.

Johnson, Sue. Hold Me Tight: Seven Conversations for a Lifetime of Love: Little, Brown Spark, 2008.

Gottman, John. The Seven Principles for Making Marriage Work. New York: Harmony Books, 1999.

Tannen, Deborah. You Just Don't Understand: Women and Men in Conversation. Ballantine Books, 1990.

Chapter 6

Carlson, D. L., Miller, A. J., and Sassler, S. 2022. Equitable Division of Labor and Marital Satisfaction. Journal of Marriage and Family, 84(1), 45–61.

Dew, J., and Stewart, R. 2019. Financial Conflict as a Predictor of Divorce: A Longitudinal Study. Journal of Family and Economic Issues, 40(2), 178–192.

Fincham, F. D., & Beach, S. R. 2021. Conflict Resolution in Marriage: A Psychological Perspective. Journal of Social and Personal Relationships, 38(4), 785–808.

Gottman, J., & Silver, N. (2022). The Seven Principles for Making Marriage Work. Harmony Books.

Harris, J., & Miller, T. (2024). Marriage and Trauma Recovery: The Role of Communication in Healing. Marriage & Family Review, 50(2), 237-254.

Johnson, S. M., & Zuccarini, D. (2021). Attachment and Intimacy in Marriage: A New Model for Conflict Resolution. Journal of Family Therapy, 43(3), 295-312.

Whisman, M. A., Dixon, A. E., & Johnson, D. P. 2023. Family Influence on Marital Conflict: Intergenerational Patterns and Outcomes. Journal of Marriage and Family, 85(4), 872–889.

Xu, Y., & Burleson, B. R. 2020. Cultural Differences in Conflict Resolution Among Married Couples: A Comparative Study of Eastern and Western Approaches. Intercultural Communication Research, 12(3), 314–332.

Chapter 7

Emmons, R. A., & McCullough, M. E. 2003. Counting blessings versus burdens: An experimental investigation of gratitude and subjective well-being in daily life. Journal of Personality and Social Psychology, 84(2), 377–389.

Algoe, S. B., Fredrickson, B. L., & Gable, S. L. 2013. The social functions of the emotion of gratitude via expression. Emotion, 13(4), 605–609.

Chapman, Gary. The 5 Love Languages: The Secret to Love That Lasts. Northfield Publishing, 1995.

Gottman, John. The Seven Principles for Making Marriage Work. Harmony Books, 1999.

Tannen, Deborah. You Just Don't Understand: Women and Men in Conversation. Ballantine Books, 1990.

Algoe, S. B., Gable, S. L., & Maisel, N. C. 2010. It's the Little Things: Everyday Gratitude as a Booster Shot for Romantic Relationships. Personal Relationships, 17(2), 217–233.

Gordon, A. M., Impett, E. A., Kogan, A., Oveis, C., & Keltner, D. (2012). To Have and to Hold: Gratitude Promotes Relationship Maintenance in Intimate Bonds. Journal of Personality and Social Psychology, 103(2), 257–274.

Chapter 8

Chapman, Gary. The 5 Love Languages: The Secret to Love That Lasts. Northfield Publishing, 1995.

Gottman, John. The Seven Principles for Making Marriage Work. Harmony Books, 1999.

Eggerichs, Emerson. Love and Respect: The Love She Most Desires; The Respect He Desperately Needs. Thomas Nelson, 2004.

Chapter 9

Chapman, G. 2019. The 5 Love Languages: The Secret to Love That Lasts. Northfield Publishing.

Emmons, R. A., & McCullough, M. E. 2019. Gratitude and Well-Being in Marriage: The Psychological and Spiritual Connection. Oxford University Press.

Fisher, H., Aron, A., & Brown, L. L. 2018. The Neuroscience of Romantic Love: An fMRI Study of Men and Women. Journal of Neurophysiology, 118(3), 115–123.

Gottman, J. 2021. The Seven Principles for Making Marriage Work. Harmony Books.

Johnson, S. M., & Zuccarini, D. (2021). Attachment and Intimacy in Marriage: A New Model for Conflict Resolution. Journal of Family Therapy, 43(3), 295-312.

Mahoney, A., Pargament, K. I., and DeMaris, A. 2021. Spiritual Intimacy and Relationship Satisfaction: A Study of Married Couples. Journal of Family Psychology, 35(1), 58–71.

McCullough, M. E., Root, L. M., & Cohen, A. D. 2020. Forgiveness and Relationships: Pathways to Emotional and Relational Healing. Journal of Positive Psychology, 15(6), 856–870.

Toussaint, L., Owen, A. D., and Cheadle, A. 2021. Religious and Spiritual Aspects of Forgiveness in Marriage and Their Impact on Psychological Well-Being. Journal of Family Psychology, 35(2), 298–312.

Worthington, E. L., and Scherer, M. 2018. The Science of Love and Connection: How Intimacy Shapes Relationships. Oxford University Press.

Xu, Y., & Burleson, B. R. 2020. Cultural Influences on Intimacy Expectations and Marital Satisfaction: A Cross-National Study. Journal of Cross-Cultural Psychology, 51(2), 134–156.

Chapter 10

Dew, J., & Stewart, R. (2019). The Role of Financial Conflict in Marriage and Divorce. Journal of Family and Economic Issues, 40(2), 178-192.

Mahoney, A., Pargament, K. I., & DeMaris, A. (2021). Financial Harmony and Marital Satisfaction: A Study of Christian Couples. Journal of Family Psychology, 35(3), 72-84.

Gottman, J. (2021). Money and Marriage: The Link Between Financial Conflict and Relationship Success. Harmony Books.

Emmons, R. A., & McCullough, M. E. (2020). Gratitude, Financial Well-being, and Relationship Satisfaction. Oxford University Press.

Chapter 11

Chapman, Gary. (1995). The 5 Love Languages: The Secret to Love That Lasts. Northfield Publishing.

Gottman, John. (2021). The Seven Principles for Making Marriage Work. Harmony Books.

Johnson, S. M., & Zuccarini, D. (2021). Attachment and Intimacy in Marriage: A New Model for Conflict Resolution. Journal of Family Therapy, 43(3), 295–312.

Mahoney, A., Pargament, K. I., & DeMaris, A. (2021). Spiritual Intimacy and Relationship Satisfaction: A Study of Married Couples. Journal of Family Psychology, 35(1), 58–71.

Worthington, E. L., & Scherer, M. (2018). The Science of Love and Connection: How Intimacy Shapes Relationships. Oxford University Press.

Chapter 12

Gottman, John & Silver, Nan. (2022). The Seven Principles for Making Marriage Work. Harmony Books.

Chapman, Gary. (1995). The 5 Love Languages: The Secret to Love That Lasts. Northfield Publishing.

Fincham, F. D., & Beach, S. R. (2021). Conflict Resolution in Marriage: A Psychological Perspective. Journal of Social and Personal Relationships, 38(4), 785–808.

Tannen, Deborah. (1990). You Just Don't Understand: Women and Men in Conversation. Ballantine Books.

Chapter 13

Eggerichs, Emerson. (2004). Love and Respect: The Love She Most Desires; The Respect He Desperately Needs. Thomas Nelson.

Keller, Timothy. (2011). The Meaning of Marriage: Facing the Complexities of Commitment with the Wisdom of God. Penguin Books.

Scuka, R. F. (2021). Relationship Enhancement Therapy: Healing Through Deep Connection. Routledge.

Chapman, Gary. (2022). The 5 Love Languages for Generations: How to Pass Love Down Through Your Family. Northfield Publishing.

Chapter 14

Enright, R. D., & Fitzgibbons, R. P. (2020). *Forgiveness Therapy: An Empirical Guide for Resolving Anger and Restoring Hope*. American Psychological Association.

Gottman, J., & Silver, N. (2022). *The Seven Principles for Making Marriage Work*. Harmony Books.

Johnson, S. M., & Zuccarini, D. (2021). *Attachment and Intimacy in Marriage: A New Model for Conflict Resolution*. Journal of Family Therapy, 43(3), 295-312.

McNulty, J. K. (2019). *The Dynamics of Marital Trust and Repair*. Journal of Marriage and Family Studies, 81(4), 689-702.

Toussaint, L., Worthington, E. L., & Williams, D. R. (2021). *Forgiveness and Health: Scientific Evidence and Theories Relating Forgiveness to Better Health*. Springer.

Worthington, E. L., & Scherer, M. (2018). *Forgiveness Is an Emotion-Focused Coping Strategy That Can Reduce Health Risks and Promote Health Resilience: Theory, Review, and Hypotheses*. Psychology & Health, 33(7), 805-825.

Fincham, F. D., & Beach, S. R. (2021). *Conflict Resolution in Marriage: A Psychological Perspective*. Journal of Social and Personal Relationships, 38(4), 785-808.

McCullough, M. E., Root, L. M., & Cohen, A. D. (2020). *Forgiveness and Relationships: Pathways to Emotional and Relational Healing*. Journal of Positive Psychology, 15(6), 856-870.

Toussaint, L., Owen, A. D., & Cheadle, A. (2021). *Religious and Spiritual Aspects of Forgiveness in Marriage and Their Impact on Psychological Well-Being*. Journal of Family Psychology, 35(2), 298-312.

Worthington, E. L. (2020). *The Science of Trust: Why It Matters in Marriage and How to Rebuild It After Betrayal*. Oxford University Press.

Chapter 15

Mahoney, A., Pargament, K. I., & DeMaris, A. (2021). Spiritual Intimacy and Relationship Satisfaction: A Study of Married Couples. Journal of Family Psychology, 35(1), 58–71.

Pargament, K. I. (2021). Spiritually Integrated Psychotherapy: Understanding and Addressing the Sacred. Guilford Press.

Wilcox, W. B. & Dew, J. (2020). The Dating Divide: Race and Desire in the Era of Online Romance. Oxford University Press.

Chapter 16

Keller, Timothy. (2011). The Meaning of Marriage: Facing the Complexities of Commitment with the Wisdom of God. Penguin Books.

Miles, Carrie A. (2006). The Redemption of Love: Rescuing Marriage and Sexuality from the Economics of a Fallen World. Brazos Press.

Stanley, S. (2014). Fighting for Your Marriage. Jossey-Bass.

Chapter 17

Wilcox, W. B., & Dew, J. (2020). The Dating Divide: Race and Desire in the Era of Online Romance. Oxford University Press.

Fowers, B. J. (2019). The Evolution of Love: A Theory of the Origins of Human Pair-Bonding. Cambridge University Press.

Scuka, R. F. (2021). Relationship Enhancement Therapy: Healing Through Deep Connection. Routledge.

Cherlin, A. J. (2021). The Marriage-Go-Round: The State of Marriage and the Family in America Today. Vintage.

McLanahan, S., & Beck, A. (2020). Parenting and Partnership: How Stable Marriages Influence Child Well-Being. Journal of Family Research, 42(2), 215-230.

Wilcox, B. W. (2022). Get Married: Why Americans Must Defy the Elites, Forge Strong Families, and Save Civilization. HarperCollins.

Kenny, D. A., Kashy, D. A., & Cook, W. L. (2021). Dyadic Data Analysis: Understanding Close Relationships. Guilford Press.

Chapman, G. (2022). The 5 Love Languages for Generations: How to Pass Love Down Through Your Family. Northfield Publishing.

Pargament, K. I. (2021). Spiritually Integrated Psychotherapy: Understanding and Addressing the Sacred. Guilford Press.

Amato, P. R., & James, S. (2020). Marriage, Divorce, and Children's Well-Being: New Findings on Generational Stability. Journal of Marriage and Family, 82(3), 567-585.

ABOUT THE AUTHOR

Dr. Aigbefo D. Ehihi is a seasoned pastor, military chaplain, and life coach with extensive expertise in theology, psychology, chaplaincy, and leadership. He is passionate about helping people navigate the sacred and personal aspects of life. He draws from years of ministry and service to equip individuals and couples with tools for wholeness and resilience.

He is the author of multiple inspirational works, including "Word of the Day: A Series Tailored to Inspire and Reinforce Your Daily Life" and "Hold Fast." Dr. Ehihi is dedicated to helping people grow spiritually, emotionally, and relationally through his teachings, books, and outreach. His mission is simple: Soaring lives to greater heights—one insight at a time.

MORE FROM THE AUTHOR

Dr. Aigbefo D. Ehihi, a distinguished pastor, military chaplain, and bestselling author, brings a unique approach to relationship counseling. His commitment to helping couples build lasting, purpose-driven relationships is fueled by faith, counseling expertise, and real-world insight. This unique blend empowers individuals to navigate marriage with clarity, resilience, and grace.

Driven by a life mission to *soar lives to greater heights—one insight at a time*, Dr. Ehihi continues to influence hearts and homes through his transformative teachings, military ministry, and widely acclaimed resources on life, leadership, and personal growth.

PUBLISHED BOOKS BY DR. AIGBEFO D. EHIHI

P.M.C.S.: Preventive Maintenance for Couples' Success: A transformative guide to building lasting marriages through daily, intentional care.

Hold Fast: A Story of Hope: Anchoring Your Faith in Difficult Times – A spiritual compass for remaining grounded when everything feels uncertain.

So Many Friends, So Little Friendship: A compelling reflection on nurturing meaningful relationships in a disconnected world.

Living Every Day with the Cross: This is a powerful call to embrace Christ's sacrifice as a daily guide for purposeful living, spiritual growth, and unwavering devotion.

Word of the Day: A Series Tailored to Inspire and Reinforce Your Daily Life (Volume 1 & Volume 2): This 90-day devotional is filled with spiritual insights, reflection prompts, and practical takeaways.

———

⮕ COMING SOON

The 7 Apology Languages: This book explores seven distinct apology languages, which are the ways people feel genuinely heard, healed, and valued during moments of hurt. Discover your apology language and learn how to prevent relationship breakdowns by resolving conflicts in a meaningful way.

The Silent Chapter: This innovative book explores the battles we fight in silence and the healing that becomes available when we confront them.

Too Many Leaders, Too Little Influence: This book boldly investigates influence in leadership beyond rank or authority, infused with principles of mission command and biblical truth.

When Things Fall Apart and the Center Could No Longer Hold: Where Is God? This book explores a faith-filled journey through personal collapse, divine questions, and spiritual rediscovery.

🌐 STAY CONNECTED

Website: www.aigbefoehihi.com

YouTube: @aigbefoehihi
Facebook: facebook.com/ehihidominion
Email: help@aigbefoehihi

Prevention Is Better Than a Cure.

ABOUT THE BOOK

P.M.C.S.: Preventive Maintenance for Couples' Success is a powerful, faith-centered guide created to help couples build, maintain, and strengthen their marriages before issues arise. Just as soldiers care for their gear to stay ready, couples should regularly nurture their relationships to avoid breakdowns and disconnection. Using biblical insights, real-life examples, and practical tools, Dr. Ehihi introduces the P.M.C.S. framework— a proactive, heart-centered approach to marriage based on covenant, not convenience. Whether you are newlyweds or seasoned partners, military families or civilian couples, this book helps you:
- Address challenges early before they become crises.
- Build trust, intimacy, and mutual understanding.
- Create a lasting legacy rooted in faith and love.
- Rekindle purpose, joy, and intentional partnership.